Managing the
Black Hole

Praise for Managing the Black Hole . . .

Gary Gack's *Managing the Black Hole: The Executive's Guide to Software Project Risk* provides a substantive yet refreshingly succinct tour of software project risks and remedies. This book explains the most important software project issues without 'geek-speak', using examples and metaphor readily comprehensible to those without extensive technical backgrounds. Gary has captured just the right level of depth and detail for today's busy executives, both inside and outside IT. Anyone dealing with risky software projects, whether 'buying' or 'building', will benefit from this book.

- **Tony Salvaggio**, CEO, Computer Aid, Inc.

Gary Gack's *Black Hole* is an excellent primer for anyone responsible for proposing, funding, planning or executing software or information technology projects. It contains many anecdotes and insights that help to explain why projects don't succeed. Gary suggests that trained project management professionals often times are unable or unwilling to rescue projects from undisciplined developers, unreasonable users, and other parties who may be uninterested in the process necessary to deliver the original project-scope on-schedule and within budget. The book's 'five virtues' spell out what businesses and IT leaders can do to help ensure successful projects."

- **John Davis**, Chief Information Officer

Gary Gack is an expert in six-sigma, software project management, and software quality. His new book is a solid combination of facts and insights derived from all three subjects. The book makes an important contribution to the literature and is recommended for business executives, software managers, QA personnel, and software engineers."

- **Capers Jones**, Author and President,
Capers Jones & Associates LLC

Senior managers with reporting software development teams are all too aware of the "black hole" associated with these projects. The last 20% of a project can drain enormous amount of resources and time. Gack clearly outlines the recipe for success to deliver software on time, within budget and with minimal defects. The key is to define and staff a disciplined process for estimating, planning, appraising and containing defects. Gack is right on target suggesting the need for third party resources for monitoring and measuring, which as he details will yield huge dividends to the bottom line. This is a classic case of utilizing incremental resources up front to avoid severe delays, cost overruns and many software patches. There are no silver bullets, but this book defines a path to success that should be read by any executive with software development teams."

- **John Bearden**, Former IBM Senior Engineering Manager and Current Consultant for Semiconductor Software Management

Gary Gack is a world class practitioner and a great example of effectively walking his talk. Gary makes his wealth of knowledge and experience readily available to others through his writing. This book will appeal to junior programmers, C-level executives, and all levels in between. It is a must read for anyone interested in creating and sustaining high performance IT teams that produce consistently superior results.

- **Tom Scott**, CIO and Senior VP of Operations, Spiegel Brands

This book provides an excellent overview of the challenges senior IT and operational managers face when deploying and maintaining software solutions in the 21st century. Gary's extensive experience with all phases of the software development process is evident in every page. His "Seven Deadly Sins of Software Development" will resonate with any executive who has been through a large systems deployment project. Gary provides practical guidance for avoiding these pitfalls and maximizing the chances of success for your next IT project.

- **Jerry Friedhoff**, Chief Quality and Process Officer, Broadridge SPS - Fixed Income

Praise for Managing the Black Hole . . .

Managing the Black Hole touches on the critical themes of managing software risks in today's world. Gack presents the problems in a methodical way and presents time-tested strategies for avoiding the pitfalls in clear language.

- **Michael Bragen**, Managing Partner, Software Productivity Research
Asia Pacific Corp., Ltd. (Beijing)

A must read for any C level leader or general manager who feels at the mercy of software development / IT and needs software on time and on cost with sensible business value. This book hits the mark in explaining methods of improving business results from software development projects to those not involved in the day to day world of software. It explains software improvements in terms general leaders can relate to: measurement, feedback, and repeatability and identifies reasons and cures for out of control software costs. I would hand this book out to leaders who unknowingly put software projects in impossible positions with unachievable schedules, impossible costs and lack of stakeholder satisfaction. It also provides technical leaders with language to explain software to executives.

- **Dan Galorath**, CEO, Galorath Incorporated

I've had the pleasure of working with Gary on multiple engagements over the course of several years. In doing so, I've developed a huge appreciation for his wealth of knowledge and experience in the area of software process improvement. In the early years of our six sigma deployment, we struggled to find the right fit within the IT domain. Gary's perspective changed our thinking and helped us see where the real opportunities were. Throughout this book, Gary addresses many of the problems that software development organizations are all too familiar with. However, he also attacks these issues at their very core, using the facts and data to shed light on a practical path to improvement. *Managing the Black Hole* is a must read for anyone seeking to drive meaningful, measurable improvements in a software development shop.

- **Thomas Bunge**, System Director, IT Lifecycle Management,
PNC Financial Services Group, Inc.

Managing the Black Hole

Black Hole

The Executive's Guide to Software Project Risk

Gary Gack

Business Expert Publishing
Thomson, Georgia

Business Expert Publishing

The Business Expert Publisher™

P.O. Box 1389

Thomson, GA 30824

Published by Sales Gravy Press

Printed in the United States of America

Cover Design: Dave Blaker

First Edition

ISBN-13: 978-1-935602-01-9

ISBN-10: 1-935602-01-2

Table of Contents

Table of Contents

Foreword

&

Acknowledgements

Throughout this book I have cited many different software industry benchmarks. Unless otherwise noted these benchmarks are based on material published or otherwise provided to me by Capers Jones. In some instances I have adapted his information to suit the present purposes. Capers is without doubt the world's foremost authority on software metrics. He is the author of more than a dozen books on software related topics – a partial list is included in the bibliography at the end of this book.

Special thanks go to Capers for his gracious assistance and friendship. As always I look forward to many more years of epic golf matches.

I also want to send a special thanks to a number of friends and reviewers. To Ed Lodge, a long standing advisor and confidant (fish fear him), to Milt Austin a mentor and friend for more than three decades, and to my many clients and collaborators over the years.

This book would not have been possible without the work of a great many industry gurus to learn from and build upon. The bibliography includes a few I have found most informative and influential. Doubtless there are many others worthy of mention.

Last but not least a special thanks to my wife Judy.

Suggested Approach to the Book

The Introduction sets the overall context for the book and is intended for all audiences. If you have been in the software or IT industry for some time, much of this material may be familiar – you may elect to scan briefly.

In Part 1 I provide industry benchmark data and overall impressions about what goes wrong with software projects. Again, this is intended for all audiences. Even if you have been in the industry for an extended period you may be surprised (and prehaps annoyed) by some of the aggregate statistics – many will believe "we're better than that". Perhaps you are, but unless you have solid data to prove you're better than industry benchmarks I urge you to read on – a very large majority are leaving a lot of "money on the table".

Part 2 drills down into the causes of failures and inefficiencies widely prevalent in the industry and provides additional more detailed benchmarks. Much of this is likely to be new information for many readers, especially General Managers, whose roles are not inside software and IT. If you are in the software or IT industry much (but not all) of this will sound familiar – you may elect to scan.

Part 3 deals with solutions – actions that will reduce failures and lead to dramatic improvements in quality, cost, and cycle time. One of my central theses is that significant improvements in software outcomes are critically dependent on understanding and support in the executive suite. Certainly industry experience clearly demonstrates dramatic improvement can be and often is frustrated by the absence of executive comprehension and support outside the software and IT organizations.

The topics addressed in this Part in most cases include

an Executive Sumary and a "Take-aways" section. General Management audiences not internal to software and IT organizations may elect to focus on these sections within each topic and scan or skip the detail between. The intervening detail is intended for software and IT professionals, as it is they who will necessarily act on the recommendations I provide.

I urge General Management audiences to read the Introduction to Part 3, the Executive Summary and Take-Aways in each section within Part 3, and all of *Focus on Performance* and *In Conclusion*. Software and IT Professionals are urged to read all of Part 3. Some topics, such as Critical Path Method, may be familiar to software professionals and can be scanned. Others, such as the Defect Containment econometric models, are less likely to be familiar and merit a more careful reading. Please feel free to contact me with questions, discussion, and/or objections.

Here's how the topics in Part 3 fit together:

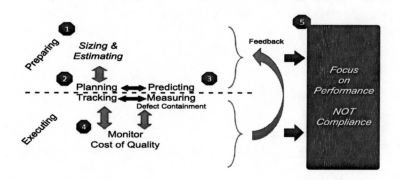

Companion Resources

This book is written for an executive level audience, but acting on the advice provided will necessarily engage the efforts of many at various levels within software provider organizations. These individuals will require a level of detail not suitable for an executive audience. To meet that need I have provided a companion web site (www.Process-Fusion.net/blackhole) that includes additional detail and links.

My company web site, www.Process-Fusion.net also provides relevant articles, white papers, recorded webinars on related topics, and information about services and training related to these topics.

In addition I offer, in conjunction with Business Expert Webinars, both live and on-demand eLearning that provides brief (1 hour) summaries of some of the topics addressed in this book. Information about scheduled events will be found at http://www.businessexpertwebinars.com/component/option,com_php/Itemid,67/user,313 – register using discount code 4981f799 for a 20% discount.

Various webinars, white papers, and eLearning programs covering software best practices and Lean Six Sigma are available through my alliance with Computer Aid University and the IT Metrics and Productivity Institute. For additional information see http://www.itmpi.org/default.aspx?pageid=509

Introduction

"Knowing is not enough; we must apply!" – **Goethe**

"In theory there is no difference between theory and practice. In practice there is." – **Yogi Berra**

First, last, and always ... **Management by Fact.** This book deals with improving business results using measurement and feedback.

Second, **Eclecticism.** There is no "one best way", no "universal solvent". Proven ingredients from disparate sources are freely blended to create a low calorie yet nourishing stew.

Third, **Pragmatism.** The book is designed for the 85% of organizations who are not today "best in class" in terms of software project results. The Software Engineering Institute and others have conducted "assessments" of software organizations for at least 20 years now and their results suggest that only about 15% of all software organizations can be considered "mature". A reasonable amount of evidence indicates those few "high maturity" organizations get significantly better results in terms of quality, cycle time, and productivity than do the other 85%.

Strategies appropriate to high maturity organizations are, in general, overkill for the 85% group. Hence, this book advocates basic blocking and tackling first, more advanced methods and strategies later. The Pareto principle certainly applies – 80% of potential gains come from 20% of potential actions. We focus here on the 20%.

Most of the nostrums discussed in this book are not new – they have been well proven for many years – but they are not universally understood and have not been widely adopted. This book offers actionable "low-calorie" adaptations of proven methods designed to close this gap.

A word about voice as used in this book. For the most part I have chosen to speak in the third person possessive – "we". I elect to do that because "we" are in this together (you and I), and because much of what I have to say here is a product of the work of many industry experts, not primarily my own. When speaking in the "we" form I have attempted to express what I believe to be a largely consensus view among those well informed about the topics covered. A short bibliography at the end of the book identifies authors I have found most influential and informative. Most of the material referenced is intended for software specialists, rather than a general management audience. When speaking in the first person singular I am speaking from my own direct experience and/ or expressing views that do not necessarily reflect a consensus of experts.

Objectives and Focus of the Book

More and more businesses and government agencies are finding software and IT to be crucial to their success and efficiency. From 'hardware' products that are becoming software-enabled to enterprise and worldwide information and business platforms – systems of software, technology, and related services drive today's organizations. This increased reliance is surfacing many shortcomings in the way software and IT is managed.

Software is central to your ability to run your business effectively – it's just as important to your success as are marketing, sales, finance, and operations. Most executives have experienced pain associated with software projects, and many have inadvertently made matters worse than they needed to be. This book will give you an MBA level of understanding of the key dynamics of software projects and will position you to improve outcomes. We deal here with management, not technology – no 'geek-speak'.

Software projects are risky – failures are common. Less than 1/3 of all software projects (purchased or built) are fully successful. Success means delivered on-time, on-budget, with the intended features and functions. The average software project overruns its budget by around 50% and schedule by around 80%. The average project delivers less than 70% of planned features and functions. These statistics have not significantly changed over at least the last 20 years!

Some may think "We buy almost all of our software – these risks don't apply to us." Sorry, the risks really aren't that much different – many failures occur when purchased software packages are deployed and when custom development is outsourced.

In particular, we are concerned with larger projects that have high cancelation risk:

- approximately 20% of projects costing $1,000,000 to $25,000,000 fail

- approximately 40% of projects costing $25,000,000 to $200,000,000 fail

    Projects in the high risk group account for around 80 - 90% of total software spending, even though they constitute only around 8-10% of all software projects.

If you have been or expect to be involved with projects in these high risk categories this book is intended for you.

Part 2 of this book provides industry benchmarks on key effectiveness metrics and examines the underlying root causes of failures – forewarned is forearmed. Leaving the solution to these problems solely in the hands of IT specialists has not proven a successful strategy – top management understanding and engagement are required to improve outcomes!

Software projects are extremely wasteful – typically only 30-40% of total software cost results in "value-added" – best in class organizations (less than 15%) achieve twice as much value add – 100% more 'bang for the buck'.

One major study conducted for the National Institute for Standards and Technology[1] quantified the impact of poor software quality – "Estimates of the economic costs of faulty software in the U.S. range in the tens of billions of dollars per year and have been estimated to represent approximately just under 1 percent of the nation's gross domestic product (GDP)."

Part 3 of this book will provide a non-technical introduction to a range of proven methods that will, with the support of key executives, enable your organization to join the elite few who have taken these lessons to heart. These proven solutions rely on facts, data, and proven management strategies primarily – technologies play a small supporting part. To paraphrase Fred Brooks, "Many silver bullets have been fired, but few dead wolves have been counted."[2]

We know of no other area of economic activity where the value-added proportion is so low. A primary goal in this book is to explain to both business executives and technologists why this is the case, and what can be done about it.

Intended Audiences

This short book is intended for a general management audience – those to whom software and IT groups report, and for software project "customers" whose interests are materially impacted. This group includes many C-level and VP level executives, and in many cases Director level as well – some inside the software/IT function, many in "the business". The approach is deliberately non-technical, yet is a substantive examination of key issues.

Business, Government, and Defense Executives, both inside and outside the technology organizations. Our experiences convince us that significant improvement in productivity, quality, and time to market requires understanding and sustained commitment from key managers on both sides of the "technology divide". This book is written in a style that is accessible to those without specific experience in software and IT development, acquisition, deployment, operations, and support. We deal with management issues, not technology.

Software, Engineering, and IT Organization Leadership at all levels – CIOs, Vice Presidents, Directors, Engineering Leaders, Project Managers, and Senior Technical Leaders. Our goal for technology practitioners is to offer a broader perspective than that typically provided to these audiences. We offer suggestions and rationale that will help software, engineering, and IT professionals communicate more effectively with business executives whose support and understanding is so essential to success. This book offers a view of the forest as seen from a distance, rather than the trees of day to day experience.

Software is Ubiquitous

Software has become an integral part of day to day life – everyone living in an advanced economy interacts with software constantly. Upscale vehicles today embody perhaps a dozen micro-processors containing millions of software instructions that control the anti-lock brakes, the fuel injection, GPS guidance system - virtually every electronically based instrument and control. Traffic lights are controlled by software; police and emergency services are dispatched and tracked by software. Airplanes, radars, air conditioning systems, ATMs, cell phones, many types of medical equipment, essentially the entire banking system, stock exchanges, CD players – software is literally everywhere.

Some of it is in the form of "applications" such as Microsoft Word or Intuit's Quicken. Much of it is invisibly 'embedded' in everyday products. We believe it is fair to say that software is the primary source of product and service differentiation, and the source of most competitive advantage. Certainly it is true that virtually all electronic and mechanical systems today are built from standard off-the-shelf components that are in most instances 'commodities' available to anyone – control of most devices and operation of most services are enabled and supported by software and IT systems.

Yet, surprisingly, many executives remain aloof from the management issues inherent in these 'mysterious' technologies. We assert that the time has come when no corporate officer or other high level manager can afford to remain largely unaware of and unengaged in the pressing issues that virtually every business faces.

Technologists alone have not, and cannot, solve the many problems of quality, cost, and cycle time that are endemic in software.

Software comes in many sizes, shapes and flavors, including:

Software products: Sometimes sold shrink-wrapped, sometimes leased, sold as a service (the "Software as a Service" model), and sometimes packaged with hardware or with consulting services. Included in this category are large "ERP" systems such as SAP and Oracle Financials as well as office automation products such as the Microsoft Office suite. Many highly specialized categories such as statistical software and design automation tools also fit here. Some items in this category are referred to as "systems software" that is "hidden" within application software more visible to the end user.

Software services: Provided by firms like IBM and outsourcers such as Tata, these services include consulting and systems design, systems integration, contract programming and systems maintenance.

In-house software: Developed traditionally by corporate IT departments to achieve cost reduction in the operations of the business (payroll, accounts receivable, manufacturing automation, etc.), but increasingly central to strategic efforts to offer a wider range of products and services which are more responsive to the customer. This category includes the sometimes extensive customization and interfacing required to integrate purchased software with legacy applications.

Embedded software: Part of a product or service, but not sold separately as software. Includes, for example, software bundled with a computer system, the on-board systems in an airplane or automobile, the code in a Nintendo or Sega game, the "browser" for an on-line service, the program within a cellular telephone, the control software in your air conditioning system.

"As software spreads from computers to the engines of automobiles to robots in factories to X-ray machines in hospitals, defects are no longer a problem to be managed. They have to be predicted and excised. Otherwise, unanticipated uses will lead to unintended consequences. For proof, look no further than the cancer patients in Panama who died after being overdosed by a Cobalt-60 radiotherapy machine. Or ask the technicians who plugged data into the software that guided that machine, and are now charged with second-degree murder."

Case Study 108, Panama's Cancer Institute

Baseline, March 2004

http://www.baselinemag.com/article2/0,1540,1543679,00.asp

Software and IT Spending

Unfortunately, the terms "software development" and "IT" (Information Technology) are used very loosely and are variously construed. In some domains the term "Systems Engineering" is also used to include some of the same activities. In general, Systems Engineering encompasses software, hardware, and humans - it is concerned with the allocation of roles and responsibilities to each.

The term "IT" is often used to include all the activities and functions that commonly fall under the auspices of the Chief Information Officer (CIO) and will generally include all aspects of acquisition, operation, and support of computers, networks, and application software. When we use the term "IT" in this book we are referring to all of these things except software development and maintenance, which for many reasons present a different set of challenges and issues.

While there are wide variations across various industries, a typical distribution of IT spending for a large US organization[3] is similar to that illustrated in the following figure:

Typical IT Organization Spending (% of Total)

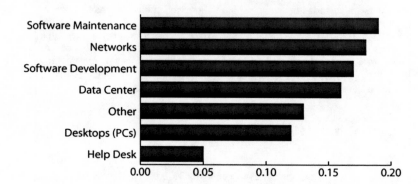

Note from the above that desktops represent only 12% of overall IT spending, while the combination of software development and maintenance accounts for more than 1/3 of total spending for a typical IT organization – about twice as much as any other single category. Software maintenance costs are to a great extent a consequence of shortcomings in the original development of the software – hence these two activities are inextricably connected.

Opportunities for improvement in software development and maintenance are far larger than they are in practically any area of business, and certainly much larger than in any other area of IT. Software issues are less tractable, more long-standing, and therefore require more attention than do issues specific to other areas of IT. Our focus here is on software – whether you build it or buy it – because that's where risk, spending, and waste are of most concern.

The next table approximates my estimates of the monetary value of the improvement opportunity typical among Fortune 500 firms. Most organizations with revenues in excess of $1 billion will find similar opportunities in proportion to their size. The hypothetical illustrations shown here were selected because they are approximate revenue mid-points among Fortune 500 companies in the indicated industry segments – other than the revenue numbers the other values in the table are speculative (but reasonable/conservative) estimates that are intended solely to give a rough magnitude value for "average opportunity" improvement potentials. This table assumes 50% of software effort is non-value-added – many experience 60-70%.

Software "Non-Value Added"	Representative Fortune 500 Companies, Selected Industries		
	Energy	Pharma	Banking
Annual Revenue (2007)	$51,000,000,000	$41,000,000,000	$24,000,000,000
Average IT%	3.3%	4.6%	9.0%
Total IT Spend	$1,679,940,000	$1,881,900,000	$2,160,000,000
Avg Software Related $ @35%	$587,979,000	$658,665,000	$756,000,000
Avg Non-Value Added $ @ 50%	$293,989,500	$329,332,500	$378,000,000
Best in Class Non-Value Added $ @25%	$146,994,750	$164,666,250	$189,000,000
Average Opportunity $	$146,994,750	$164,666,250	$189,000,000

In many industries the potential for improvement in an "average" Fortune 500 company exceeds $150,000,000 annually. This opportunity can be 'harvested' as either reduced cost or additional delivered software. In firms whose principal product is software, the potential (as a share of revenue) is far greater. One might suppose such firms are far more efficient, but available evidence suggests that is only marginally the case – for most, time to market dominates, not efficiency. The time /cost trade-off for software is very steep and not well understood by most decision makers – we will explore that more fully as we progress.

The Economic Significance of Software

Sources of statistical information about the impact of software on the economy are closely held and expensive to obtain from firms such as Gartner and Forester. We rely here on a variety of sources that are in the public domain. Information about "Software Publishers" (NAICS 51121) is somewhat more readily available than is information about custom programming and design service (NAICS 541511 and 541512). All of the available data require certain adjustments to reflect "reality" as I perceive it from more than 40 years experience in the field - I readily acknowledge there is room for argument about the assumptions I make.

The effort and cost devoted to software development and maintenance done by "in-house" personnel in banks and other firms, rather than by firms specifically in the software business, is very difficult to estimate with certainty. I believe in most large firms somewhere between 50 and 75% of all software maintenance and development is done "in-house" – hence, my overall assumption is that the in-house portion is at least 50% of total software spending.

As of May, 2006 I estimated over 2.8 million individuals in the US were directly employed in software development and maintenance, and this is likely understated as these numbers do not include government employees, military personnel or other individuals who actually do software work but carry other titles not included here. This total represented about 2.1% of total US non-farm employment, and nearly 17% of professional and business services employment. Nearly $200 billion in annual earnings were attributable to these individuals – roughly 4.4% of total national earnings from employment.

U.S Bureau of Labor Statistics	Employment (2006)	Median Earnings (2006)
Total US Employment, Median Earnings	2,815,600	$71,110
Software Engineers	857,000	$79,780
Programmers	435,000	$65,510
Systems Analysts	504,000	$69,760
Computer/Information Systems Mgrs.	264,000	$101,580
Database Administrators	119,000	$64,670
Support Specialists (est. 30%)	258,600	$41,470
"Engineers" (est.25%)	378,000	$75,000

Notes: (1) Support specialists are an indispensible part of software development and maintenance – I estimate 30% of the total are primarily associated with software development and maintenance. (2) Many engineers develop software as their principal activity, but are not classified in software related position titles. I estimate 25% of total engineering effort is actually software related.

An additional perspective on the economic significance of software can be seen from the US 2002 Economic Census[4], as summarized below. These data reflect a survey of over 98,000 "establishments" (locations within companies) primarily engaged in the indicated sectors of the software industry. These data do not reflect software activities within firms not primarily in the software business. "Employees" in this table refers to total employment in these establishments, of which those actually engaged in software development and maintenance are a subset. While large variance is common, I estimate approximately 30% of these employees, about 370,000, were actually engaged in software development and maintenance, with the remainder in sales, support, administration, finance, and other activities.

2002 US Economic Census	Businesses	Sales	Employees	Payroll
Total Software	98,423	$242 Billion	1,230,690	$94 Billion
51121 Software Publishers	9,953	$102 Billion	356,708	$35 Billion
541511 Custom	48,953	$60 Billion	439,395	$30 Billion
541512 Computer Systems Design Services	39,517	$78 Billion	434,587	$29 Billion

One additional source provides a valuable perspective. The Top 100 Foundation[5], based in the Netherlands, produces an annual survey, *Software Top 100 – The World's Largest Software Companies.* This survey, which includes "packaged" (published) software only, attempts to tease out the portion of software related sales of large diversified companies such as IBM and HP. These 100 companies collectively had estimated sales of over US$203 billion for the calendar year 2008, of which approximately 87% is attributable to US owned firms. These 100 firms collectively account for around 95% of total software sales. This appears to account for roughly 80% of total published software sales reported by the US Economic Census. The remaining 20% is most likely software sold as an integrated element of another product rather than as a separate item.

Part One

Part One
What Goes Wrong
(The Grim Realities)

Alfred's not worried about the success of your software project (it's not his money), but most likely many of you with a big stake in a software project are worried, and with reason. Certainly the industry data are pretty depressing - we'll begin by putting things into perspective – chances are you don't have solid numbers like those we'll describe, but it's very likely the story in your organization is pretty similar.

What, Me Worry?

Introduction to Part One – "What Goes Wrong"

In Part 1 we examine the "grim realities" of software projects and organizations as they are today among the immature 85%. We review industry benchmarks that quantify failure rates and the amazing level of waste that is endemic in the industry.

We examine the central role of quality in software economics, consider a "systems dynamics" model of a typical software project, and relate software projects to Peter Senge's "Laws".

We then consider the role of knowledge and "knowing – doing" gaps as important contributors to the current state of affairs.

Software: An Immature Industry

Many in the technical end of the software industry are highly specialized and focus on relatively narrow areas of expertise. The management end of the software business is nearly the opposite – too little specialization, especially in the areas of estimating, defect containment, and effectiveness and efficiency metrics.

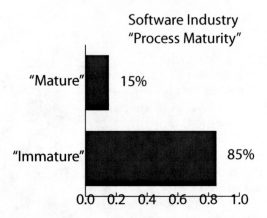

Much emphasis has been placed on collective organization level assessment of software "process capability", and those sorts of assessments are the basis for my assertion that around 85% are "immature". One scheme of classifying the "capability" of software groups, called "Process Capability/Maturity level", is based on an assessment scheme developed by the Software Engineering Institute (SEI). It is based on Phil Crosby's "Quality Maturity Grid" from TQM days.

Known as the "Capability Maturity Model Integrated" (CMMI®) it is a 5-level rating scheme that reflects the extent to which an organization has defined and repeatable processes that achieve specified goals and embody specified practices. Like ISO, it is a "compliance-based" approach to improvement and does not explicitly measure actual performance – it assumes, supported by some evidence, that an appropriate set of defined processes lead to improved performance.

Most of the high-maturity 15% are found in aerospace and government contractor organizations, where high maturity is essentially mandatory. This book is geared to the 85% - if you are fortunate to be among the select 15% group, you probably already understand and apply many of the ideas we cover here.

A word of caution – pursuing "process maturity" for its own sake can be very expensive. Getting certified to SEI level 3 can cost $2-$3,000,000 (and will very possibly decrease your productivity in the near term). Our focus here is on "performance-based" improvement. High maturity is not, in itself, a guarantee of outstanding performance.

Speaking of performance, here's some sobering industry data – only about 30% of software projects are fully successful (on-time, on-budget, complete). These data have been collected for about 15 years now, and as we see in this subset, the success rate has changed very little.

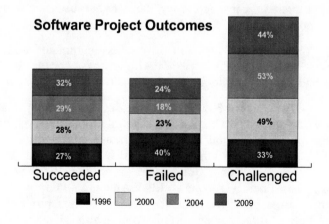

(Source: The Standish Group)

When we look at where software project money actually goes in the 85% organizations, it's even more depressing.

Where Your Software $ Goes

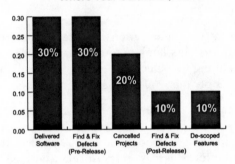

Only 30% is actually spent building software – 30% more goes to finding and fixing defects before the product is delivered, and another 10% is required to fix defects after the product is installed and in use. Clearly it is necessary to do testing and fix the bugs, but does anyone really want to spend more money on that than on building software in the first place?

An additional 20%, on average, is spent on projects that are never completed – cancelled along the way because they're over budget, no longer needed, or whatever.

The remaining 10% is spent on partially completed features and functions that are de-scoped later in a project because it's behind schedule or over budget.

In total, only about 30% of total cost delivers anything that is truly "value-added". **Value Added** is simply total time spent minus time spent on Appraisal, Rework, undelivered features, and cancelled projects. When measured, which rarely occurs, Value Added is commonly 30% of total effort. Improving efficiency, simply put, means increasing value added! Any and all improvement initiatives can set goals and measure improvements in terms of impact on Value Added – which occurs when Appraisal and Rework are reduced.

Note that this definition of Value Added is offered for the sake of "operational definition" simplicity – it does not exclude the possibility that some effort categorized as Value Added may by redundant or unnecessary. However, let's eat the elephant one bite at a time – when we get Value Added to 50% or less we can begin to consider refinements of our categories.

Appraisal is all time spent *finding* defects – in most organizations this is primarily testing, but may also include inspections and reviews of various work products prior to testing. Most organizations plan to devote 30-40% of total effort to this activity, but usually have no idea if that is enough or too much. Testing usually stops when time runs out with little or no insight into the effectiveness of effort expended. Appraisals, once you decide to do them, can be regarded as "fixed" costs – i.e., that effort will be expended even if no defects are found.

Rework is all time spent *fixing* defects found by any form of appraisal and/or by customers after a system is delivered - typically 30-40% of total effort, but rarely measured. Rework is always a *variable* cost that is a function of the number of defects actually found. To predict that you must make some estimate (implicit or explicit) of the number of defects you expect to find.

Most organizations cannot separate Appraisal effort from Rework effort.

Schedule and cost performance is also a depressing picture – the average project in 2009 overran budget by 45%, schedule by 63% - the "good news" is, we're back to where we were in 2000. Performance will vary with size – larger is much riskier, and of course there's a lot of variance – some projects are much worse, some better.

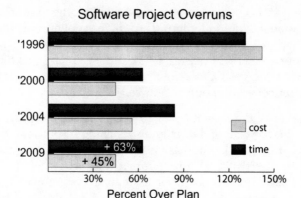

Software Project Overruns

(Source: The Standish Group)

What is your pain threshold? What can you afford? It's important to set a threshold above which more than "normal" controls and measures will be required. Obviously you can't get involved in every single project – often there are dozens going on concurrently. As we progress we'll be offering suggestions for how to recognize early that a project is off track, and how to take preventive actions before "over the threshold" projects even get started.

Focus is key – high risk projects are only 8-10% of all projects, but those few consume something like 90% of total software development spending!

Software: Quality is Key

As indicated earlier, defect detection and removal account for at least 40% of total software costs in the "85%" organizations – more than the cost of creating the software in the first place. Cancelled projects add another 20%, and features not delivered an additional 10% - in total, 70% of your software budget is waste in one form or another. I can hear the cries now – "No, no – that's not us!" Ok, maybe your waste is not 70% - maybe it's 60%, or even 50% - but if you are not one of the elite 15%, it is certainly in that range. In most areas of a well run business non-value-add is less than 20%.

It's natural to be in denial about this, but if you have not actually measured it (and only a few have) it's certainly much worse than you would imagine. It's very unlikely your current measurement systems provide any realistic understanding of your value-added to non-value-added ratio. Please, have someone independent and knowledgeable about how to do it take a look - in the long run, you'll be glad you did. You certainly won't fix it if you don't know the facts.

Fixing it will require a focus on QUALITY - we can't do it faster if we don't first learn how to do it BETTER. Quality drives both cost and schedule - the old "pick two" joke is patently false. So is the Parkinsonian notion that work expands to fill the time allocated. When it comes to software, taking time to do it right is the only way to do it faster and cheaper.

One helpful way to visualize the dynamics of software projects is to apply the sort of thinking described by Peter Senge in his seminal work, *The Fifth Discipline: The Art and Practice of the Learning Organization*[6]. Essentially, we deal here with how organizations can learn to be more effective in their management of software related projects, and many of Senge's messages apply. Senge's "systems dynamics" types of models illustrate various types of cause and effect feedback loops, one example of which is provided below. This is a very realistic depiction of what happens to many software projects.

If you are familiar with Senge's models this diagram may make sense to you, but if not it's probably a bit confusing. Each of the numbered steps is briefly described below the diagram to clarify my intent.

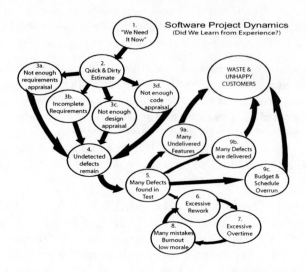

1. "We Need It Now" – many projects begin with a great sense of urgency.

2. Often that urgency leads to "quick and dirty" estimates that prove to be unrealistic.

3. Four important consequences flow from the initial unrealistic estimate:

    a. Insufficient time is devoted to checking the requirements for correctness and clarity.

    b. Requirements tend to be incomplete – important needs are missed – key stakeholders are not included – we don't have time to do it right, but we'll find time to do it over later.

    c. Insufficient time is devoted to checking the design to ensure it is complete, correct, and fully consistent with the requirements.

    d. The "code" that translates the design into "computer language" is not sufficiently reviewed and validated to ensure it is correct and fully consistent with the design.

4. Many undetected defects remain.

5. Many defects are found during testing – far more than expected – the expected final 1/3 of the project schedule becomes 2/3.

6. The larger than expected number of defects detected during testing means much greater than expected rework.

7. The software team starts working 80 hour weeks.

8. They make even more mistakes, leading to even more rework. After several weeks or months of this burnout sets in, morale plummets. Repeat 6 thru 8 until the project is cancelled or delivered with many defects.

9. IF the project gets delivered many unhappy consequences remain.

    a. Many features originally intended to be included are dropped.

    b. The delivered product contains many defects impacting both users and support groups.

    c. The schedule and budget are greatly exceeded.

The end result: Lots of WASTE and UNHAPPY CUSTOMERS

(The software team isn't very happy either!)

Senge formulated eleven "laws" of the Fifth Discipline, all of which directly apply to software projects (*examples in italics*):

1. Today's problems come from yesterday's "solutions" – *last year we introduced new software tools and methods designed to improve productivity.*

2. The harder you push, the harder the system pushes back – *now we have more staff dedicated to maintaining the tools and methods.*

3. Behavior grows better before it grows worse – *everybody loved it at first … but productivity has not measurably improved.*

4. The easy way out usually leads back in – *we'll buy some new tools, try a new method.*

5. The cure can be worse than the disease – *introducing new tools and methods always has a learning curve.*

6. Faster is slower- *compressed schedules (#2 in the diagram) lead to shortcuts, which always lead to more rework later – slow down at the beginning to get it right.*

7. Cause and effect are not closely related in time and space – *projects often last a year or more – nobody remembers the original sins, or learns from them.*

8. Small changes can produce big results – but the areas of highest leverage are often least obvious – *proven appraisal methods applied early can reduce defect discovery and repair costs by a factor of at least 5.*

9. You can have your cake and eat it too, but not at once – *patience is a virtue – rush now, pay a lot later.*

10. Dividing an elephant in half does not produce two small elephants – *"agile" methods (building systems in very small chunks) are NOT the holy grail for high risk projects.*

11. There is no blame – *get over it! Exiles to the gulag don't work – the next wizard won't do better than the last unless the dynamics are changed!*

The Knowledge Gap

"There are some people who, if they don't already know, you can't tell 'em." – Yogi Berra

These grim realities are a consequence of several different kinds of knowledge gaps. Some of these gaps reside in the executive suite – these are the primary focus of this book – we provide the essential knowledge this audience needs, explained in plain English. There really is no reason to expect executives would be aware of the issues and ideas we address, but it is clear that absent the necessary core ideas it is highly unlikely the underlying problems will be effectively addressed – understanding necessarily precedes effective action.

Additional, and equally critical, knowledge gaps reside inside the software/IT function in most organizations. Depending on the role of a given individual they will generally be very well versed in a range of fairly exotic topics – they may have deep knowledge of certain aspects of business processes, such as the order to cash cycle. Some may be intimately acquainted with the inner workings of obscure technologies and languages – the realm of 'geek-speak'. All of this knowledge is absolutely essential – software and IT does not work without these sorts of highly specialized expertise in complex topics. All of this vast array of 'technical' knowledge is absolutely necessary – but not sufficient.

All of this technical stuff is constantly changing – almost hourly. No wonder most of these folks are barely able to keep up with the technical essentials they absolutely must possess to do the job every day. We should not be surprised that many of them have little awareness (if even an interest) in the types of metrics and management issues that are the focus of this book. In part as a consequence of this widespread knowledge gap on management topics within the software/IT community, resistance to and skepticism about many of these ideas abound. Within the software/IT community this knowledge gap is not widely recognized or acknowledged. It is, nonetheless, a fact. This book will provide the essential knowledge required by both groups.

These knowledge gaps are actually not difficult to close – but that's the easy part – the real challenge is closing the "knowing-doing" gap. Without help from the executive suite, that just won't happen.

The "Knowing-Doing" Gap

Pfeffer and Sutton's excellent book[7] (worth a read quite aside from its relevance to our concerns here) is the result of "an intensive long-term research effort to discover what prevented organizations that are led by smart people from doing things that they know they ought to do." As indicated above, the challenge in software/IT is in part a lack of knowledge, but even when that knowledge is at hand it often does not lead to effective action.

I'll not attempt to do justice to all of their analysis and advice, but perhaps a few key points are especially relevant here, along with commentary (in italics) as it relates to our current topic:

- "We found no simple answers to the knowing-doing dilemma." *Similarly this book has no magical solutions to every management issue in software and IT, but it does offer practical suggestions to address a few of the most pressing problems. As always, acting with 'brain-engaged' is necessary to adapt general advice to specific situations.*

- "One of the most important insights from our research is that knowledge that is actually implemented is much more likely to be acquired by doing than from learning or reading, listening, or even thinking." *As Yoda said, "try not – do!"*

- "Spend less time just contemplating and talking about organizational problems. Taking action will generate experience from which you can learn." *Part 3 of this book proposes a specific set of 'low-calorie' actions that, if taken, will generate learning and improved results – a runaway snowball effect if you will give it a push to get it started and an occasional nudge over the rough spots.*

- **"Great companies get remarkable performance from ordinary people."** *Certainly it makes sense to hire the best you can get, but everyone does that. Make the best possible use of those you have. Everything suggested here is doable with an average workforce and does not require large investment (indeed, the actions suggested will pay for themselves in very short order.)*

- **"One important reason we discovered for the knowing-doing gap is that companies over-estimate the importance of the tangible, specific, programmatic aspects of what competitors, for instance, do, and under-estimate the importance of underlying philosophy that guides what they do and why they do it."** *Two philosophies are key to success in software and IT – (1) Quality comes first – doing it right the first time saves money and time (2) Senge's "Law" #6 "Faster is slower" applies to every software project – make sure estimates are realistic, and effort is spent early to find the defects. Don't make unrealistic demands that lead to 'unnatural acts'.*

Part One "Take-aways"

- The software industry is immature – only about 15% of all software organizations can be considered "best in class" (and even that group are not entirely immune to failure).

- Less than 1/3 of software projects are fully successful – delivered on time, on budget, with all promised functionality.

- An average organization among the immature 85% experiences a "non-value-added" rate in the area of 60-70% of total software spending.

- Reducing non-value added effort REQUIRES a focus on quality. Quality drives both cost and schedule.

- Software project dynamics can be modeled using the "systems dynamics" convention described by Peter Senge.

- Both knowledge gaps and "knowing-doing" gaps contribute to software project shortcomings.

---

[1]The Economic Impacts of Inadequate Infrastructure for Software Testing, NIST Planning Report 02-3

[2]Brooks, Frederick P., "No Silver Bullet: Essence and Accidents of Software Engineering," Computer, Vol. 20, No. 4 (April 1987) pp. 10-19.

[3]For details on this topic, see http://www.gartner.com

[4]Source:http://factfinder.census.gov/servlet/SAFFSelectIndustry?_event=&geo_id=01000US&_geoContext=01000US&_street=&_county=&_cityTown=&_state=&_zip=&_lang=en&_sse=on&ActiveGeoDiv=&_useEV=&pctxt=bg&pgsl=010&_submenuId=business_2&ds_name=null&_ci_nbr=null&qr_name=null&reg=null%3Anull&_keyword=software&_industry=

[5] See http://www.softwaretop100.org/index.php

[6]The Fifth Discipline, Peter Senge, Doubleday 1990 ISBN 0-385-26094-6

[7]The Knowing – Doing Gap: How Smart Companies Turn Knowledge Into Action, Jeffrey Pfeffer and Robert Sutton, Harvard Business School Press, 2000 ISBN 1-57851-124-0

Part Two

Part Two
Why Software Projects and Organizations Fail
(Seven Deadly Sins)

"The Seven Deadly Sins stem from the same beast. Pride wrapped in his own world of self admiration, Greed has his one track mind on owning what he can while Envy eyeballs his goods. Wrath is completely consumed in fiery blindness while Lust, Gluttony and Sloth live like parasites and feed upon this beastly serpent."

by Valerie Majer, 2005 (with permission)

While parallels between morality and software are inexact, software projects and organizations often stray onto the road to perdition, committing sins of omission and commission. Many search for salvation in places it is unlikely to be found.

Introduction to Part Two:

Why Software Projects and Organizations Fail

In this part of the book my goal is to examine the most common reasons software projects fail and why the immature 85% software organizations are not making much progress in the direction of improvement. Understanding the real state of affairs and some of the fundamental dynamics and metrics is a necessary pre-condition to effective action. In Part 3 we will consider what to do about the issues discussed in Part 2.

Some of my reviewers felt it would be better to follow each "what goes wrong" topic with a corresponding solution discussion. Because the various reasons for failure, and the solutions, are highly inter-connected I have elected to separate causes from solutions. I believe it is best to understand the full scope of the problem before we entertain solutions.

For convenience we can group the seven deadly sins into two broad categories.

Preparing

- Risk Recognition

- Sizing and Estimating

- Project Planning

Executing

- Methods, Standards, and Tools

- Product Quality

- Measurement

- Status Reporting

The first deadly sin deals with **Risk Recognition**, where we examine industry data on costs and risks of significant software projects. Few executive decision makers really understand what they are getting into and are often unduly optimistic.

Sizing and Estimating, the second deadly sin, examines benchmark data on the current grim realities and explains the fundamentals of the dynamic relationship among effort (cost), duration, and delivered quality. By analogy we examine common misconceptions that lead to unrealistic estimates and schedules.

Deadly sin number three deals with widespread inadequacies in **Planning.**

The fourth deadly sin we will explore relates to the unending quest for "the best" **Methods, Standards, and Tools.** As we will see, many organizations expend a great deal of effort attempting to deploy complex standards and methods without a clear understanding of the difference between "compliance" and "performance". Many of these standards and methods do offer something of value, but they are typically effective for the mature 15%, not for the immature 85%.

We also examine the "silver bullet syndrome" – a widespread industry tendency to believe in tools as magic wands. Tools, unfortunately, do not make the software engineer into a wizard. As Tim Lister has pointed out, "A fool with tool is still a fool."

Deadly sin number five relates to software **Product Quality** issues. Measuring and managing software quality is the single most important action that can be taken to improve outcomes. It's not rocket science, but the state of practice among the 85% is pretty dismal. Fixing it is not difficult or expensive. In Part 3 we will examine what needs to be done, but understanding comes first.

Measurement, deadly sin number six, is central to real progress. Many of the 85% organizations have a lot of measures today, but most are not very useful. Here we define what is needed, and what's wrong with the data most groups have now. As we will see, "less is more".

Sin seven deals with **Status Reporting**. Few among the 85% have realistic reports of progress.

Risk Recognition

Many organizations undertake projects without understanding the level of risk involved. Starting a software project is a bit like a trip to Las Vegas – it's a good idea to decide before you start how much you can afford to lose. A $100 billion multi-national might not notice a $10 million project failure, but if you're a $500 million mid-market firm your pain threshold is probably a lot lower. Risks come in several distinct flavors:

- Inherent risks

- Innovation risks

- Capability risks

- Commitment risks

Any of these risks alone can cause a failure, and when more than one is in play failure is nearly inevitable. **Inherent risks** are largely a function of the size of a project. Here are a few examples of projects in broad size ranges.

Size	Examples
Very Large	U.S. Air Traffic Control, SAP, Aegis Destroyer Command & Control, Microsoft XP
Large	Airline Reservation System, FBI Fingerprint Analysis, American Express Billing
Medium	Bank ATM Controls, Norton Anti-Virus, PBX Switching System
Small	Auto Fuel Injection, Anti Lock Brake Controls

Systems in these size classes will generally cost somewhere in the ranges indicated in the table below. "Function Points" are one of the more commonly used methods of sizing software projects.

Approximate Cost by Size Range			
Size	"Function Points"	Typical Cost Range US$	
Very Large	100,000 +	$550 Million	$1.2 Billion
Large	10,000–100,000	$25 Million	$200 Million
Medium	1,000 – 10,000	$1.0 Million	$25 Million
Small	< 1,000	$100,000	$800,000

Adapted from Capers Jones © 2007

Although "small" projects account for 80-90% of the total number of projects across the industry, they account for only around 10% of total cost. Medium and Large projects are perhaps 8-10% of the total number of projects, but account for at least 80% of total spending.

Systems at the larger end of this scale have greatly increased probabilities of cancellation, as indicated by the following graph.

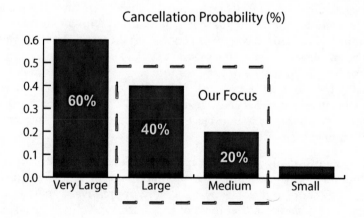

A typical multi-national firm will have hundreds or thousands of systems in the medium range and dozens to hundreds in the large category. Outside of government, defense, and industries that supply software infrastructure (such as operating systems provided by Microsoft, IBM and others) few firms will build systems in the very large category. Far more likely systems in that category, such as SAP, will be purchased. Many of the risks and issues we discuss here apply equally to deployments of very large purchased systems such as SAP.

Innovation risks arise when projects are on the "bleeding edge" where something is being undertaken that has not been done before. Some of these risks relate to use of new technologies such as neural networks or artificial intelligence. Some involve implementation of functionality not previously attempted – e.g., the infamous Denver Airport Baggage System.

Innovation risks and capability risks often interact. **Capability risks** relate to the actual capability of the project team to successfully undertake a project comparable to the one proposed as *demonstrated by past success*. Capability has a number of dimensions. The team must include a sufficient number of persons who understand the application domain – e.g., experience with large scale banking systems does not qualify one to create avionics software. The team must include a sufficient number of individuals with proven expertise in the methods, technologies, tools, and management strategies to be employed – again, demonstrated prior success. Many failures arise because a new team decides to use a technology or method that is new to most of the team. When this occurs, learning curve risk is introduced. Especially critical is demonstrated prior success in key positions such as project management, quality assurance, estimating, architecture, etc.

One especially prevalent capability risk arises in outsourcing situations. While certainly it is true that major outsourcing firms, both off- shore and domestic, have very impressive corporate resumes, it is also true that most of these firms have high turnover rates and teams often include many who are comparatively junior.

Commitment risks arise when the "customer" fails to adequately engage with the developer. Key people are too busy to participate in requirements gathering processes. They don't have time to review draft specifications in sufficient detail. "That's not my job – let the IT guys figure this out." EVERY significant software project will require a substantial (often full time) commitment of some of the best and most knowledgeable people in the customer organization. The ones who are the busiest are those most needed to ensure success. Significant engagement will be required throughout the project – "once and done" is never enough for larger projects. Lack of adequate customer commitment and engagement is a contributing factor in at least half of all software project failures.

Lack of an engaged executive sponsor is a root cause for many software project failures. If an executive who wants a project is not willing to commit a significant amount of time of key staff, the project is unlikely to succeed. In most of my turnaround work this is a factor.

Sizing and Estimating

We want it all, and we want it now! **Wishful thinking** is positively an epidemic – leaders at every level fall victim. In my experience, certainly supported by industry data, wishful thinking is a result of a variety of factors, but lack of estimating expertise is the most serious. Machismo plays a part as well – even if no one else has ever done "it" that fast, we can!

With few exceptions, both inside and outside IT, most of those involved simply don't know how to reliably determine a realistic and attainable budget and schedule – it's a dark art that few really understand. Schedules and budgets get set by guesswork and mandate, and they're almost always too low. Beware misleading status reports – we often hear claims a project was "on-time" and "on-budget" when it actually delivered 2/3 of the planned features – objectively viewed, that is in fact a 50% overrun. In Part 3 we'll discuss how to set up "size-adjusted" metrics of success.

The 3-Minute Mile

A typical estimating scenario goes something like this:

"We seem to go through the same drill with schedule and budget commitments every time. Our customers insist, understandably, that we provide a preliminary estimate of project costs and schedule very early in the process before anybody really knows what the requirements and scope actually are. We give them our best guess, always making sure we tell them it's a guess. Once we have a signed-off statement of user requirements[1] we go through a careful planning process and come up with a much more realistic estimate of effort and schedule. Our manager takes that to the customer and inevitably comes back and tells us we have to stick with the original guess! Of course we never make it and we're made out to be the bad guys! We're all really fed up with this – what can we do about it?"

Anchoring Schedules in the Real World

Ouch! Everybody who's been doing software projects for even a short while has probably experienced this.

We all realize estimating interacts with requirements issues (when requirements change so do estimates), but for the sake of clarity we will treat the estimating problem in isolation. Software cost estimating is fraught with all sorts of difficulties, but under the complexity there are some universal truths that are worth understanding. Simplified analogies, so long as they are faithful to reality, can sometimes help us manage customer and management expectations more realistically than might otherwise be possible.

One analogy familiar to everyone, and yet faithful to the real dynamics of software projects, relates to costs and risks associated with vehicle transportation. In these days of high fuel prices, some of us might be thinking more carefully than in the past about the pros and cons of taking the family on a driving vacation in that new SUV.

Perhaps the spouse and kids have always wanted to see the Grand Canyon – a pretty long trip from our home in Florida – about 2500 miles each way. The boss has given us a 2 week vacation, so we've got to work within that time frame – similar to a fixed deadline for a software project. Also like a software project (sometimes) the essential requirements are not negotiable – spouse and all three kids are coming along – leaving somebody home is not an option. We do have a bit of flex about what we take with us, so to some small degree we can control the weight of our vehicle.

We need to make a pretty good estimate of what this trip is likely to cost – braces for Susie and tuition for Chelsea are putting a dent in our available funds. So, we need to consider our time limit and the expenses involved. Like software projects, these factors are interdependent – i.e., what it will cost (fuel, maintenance, etc) is in part a function of how fast we drive and how much stuff (scope of the requirements) we bring along. And how fast we drive impacts how much time we'll be able to spend actually vacationing (reaping the benefits) and how much time we'll spend driving in the car. Hmmm ... this is getting a little difficult to envision without writing it all down to clarify what our options are and calculating the consequences of the various options available.

We might prepare an analysis something like the following, using 5,000 miles round trip and fuel at $3.00 per gallon:

Speed (MPH)	Weight (Rqmts Scope)	Drive Time (Duration)	Miles/Gallon (Productivity)	Fuel Cost (Effort)	Risks
50	Nominal	100 hrs	18	$832	Nominal
60	Nominal	83 hrs	16	$938	+ (accidents)
70	Nominal	71 hrs	14	$1071	++ accidents + tickets
80	Nominal	62 hrs	12	$1,250	+++ accidents +++ tickets

We could elaborate this with more options related to weight and perhaps introduce other factors, but this is enough to get the idea. As with software cost estimating it is possible to construct scenarios that illustrate the consequences of choices open to us. Are we willing to risk tickets and accidents (delivered defects and missed schedules and budgets) in order to have some sort of chance to save 30% of the drive time (duration)? Realizing it will cost 50% more and that we will have to take into account the possible (probable) costs and delays of the tickets and repairs?

Software projects always experience exactly these fundamental dynamics, but the actual underlying models that mathematically describe these dynamics are much more complex and non-intuitive than the simple model we presented here. Yet the analogy is perfectly applicable and valid – faster costs more (a lot more) and carries greater risks – the "leverage" in software projects is far steeper than in this example.

The increases in risks and costs are dramatically non-linear (exponential) and hence have far more serious and costly consequences than is the case with our simple trip model. In reality it is often true that a 30% compression of a "least cost" schedule (50 miles per hour) will lead to 2-3x final cost and 5-8x delivered defects.

All of the proven software cost models embody non-linear relationships that are virtually impossible to visualize – models are essential to fact-based discussion. NOTE: you don't need to understand the formulas to use the "black box" tools in which they are embodied!

The take away from all of this is that in a fact-based culture where key players are quantitatively literate the idea of modeling outcomes and making decisions with brain engaged and eyes open is the norm. The 15% group behave that way, the 85% don't. As one of the reengineering gurus said, "Do what you always did, get what you always got." Organizations that understand "Management by Fact" (and use it) don't try to run 3-minute miles when the world record is 3:40!

Facts Trump Wishes and Opinions

Constructive solutions always rest on getting, analyzing, and acting on facts – not on fault-finding, finger pointing, or exiles to the gulag. When appropriate values of relevant variables are not known, often the case in the early stages of deployments, it is at least possible to consider a range of worst / best / most likely.

We are, after all, always dealing with uncertainty – every decision in the world we operate in involves risk. Models won't ever give us the absolutely correct answer, but experience shows they get a lot closer than guessing!

It is very common to encounter a situation in which a business executive will dictate the schedule for a software project, frequently over-ruling the software manager who has prepared an estimate of cost and schedule. While this is quite understandable, since experience has proven these estimates are wrong more often than right, it is also true that many software project failures are directly traceable to this dynamic.

This phenomenon is often referred to as "schedule pressure". Imagine a buyer hires a contractor to build a new house – the contractor quotes a price and a tentative move in date – the buyer's response is something like "I must move in two months sooner, and I won't pay a nickel more." Does anyone imagine the contractor will accept that?

Of course not! Yet, that happens to software managers every day in many, many companies – and, for whatever reason, they usually rollover and say "yes boss". In reality the software team will virtually never deliver what was originally expected on the dictated schedule. If they do deliver on the required date, the house will be missing two rooms, it won't be painted, and the roof will leak.

Frequently, the software customer is requiring a level of performance that is simply not attainable – often the required schedule has never been achieved for a software product of the size in question.

Speed Kills

The impact of schedule pressure has been quantitatively modeled (based on databases of thousands of completed projects) by several software cost estimating tools, including Jones' KnowledgePlan (www.spr.com), Putnam's SLIM (www.qsm.com) and Galorath's SEER (www.galorath.com). All of these models clearly show non-linear (exponential) relationships among project effort, delivered quality and the schedule itself.

The impact of the schedule is particularly dramatic for larger projects (generally those greater than 10 person years of effort). For larger projects it is clear that compression of the schedule can increase cost by a factor of 2 to 3, increase delivered defects by a factor of 5 or more, and greatly increase risk of failure. In larger projects you can realistically expect to get 3 for the price of 2 if you opt for least cost schedules – in a typical case that may mean 12 months instead of 9 (which probably won't happen anyway).

In other words, a project that could be delivered in 12 months at a cost of around $1,000,000 may cost $2,000,000 or more to deliver in 9 months, and the quality will be dramatically lower. This is not speculation, but as near as we get to universal truth in software.

Software projects fall into this trap very frequently – actually far more often than not. Software types tend to be optimists, and leaders tend to be in a hurry – a deadly combination that leads to planned schedules and budgets that never had any chance to be realized. In my turnaround work at least 80% of the time a totally unrealistic initial estimate is one of the major contributing factors causing software train wrecks. Software cost estimating is absolutely the worst weakness in the field!

In the next few paragraphs we will explore a set of fundamental and indisputable facts about software estimating – just the essential ideas, not all of the underlying complexity. Understanding these facts can save a lot of grief if they are taken to heart.

There are several very effective software cost estimating tools on the market, and a rather small number of experts who know how to use them properly. All of these estimating models are built from databases of thousands of completed projects – they reflect what has actually proven to be possible in a wide range of contexts – different project sizes, tools, technologies, staff experience, etc., etc. The software estimating formula shown here was developed by Larry Putnam (www.QSM.com) and is one of the very few published – most models are proprietary and not published, and even Putnam's published work does not reveal the whole story. The implications of this formula are hardly intuitive, so it may come as no surprise that few really "get it" about software estimates.

Size = (Effort/ß)$^{(.33)}$ * Time$^{(1.33)}$ * Process Productivity

In the next few pages we'll explore the fundamental dynamics that are universal truths of software cost estimates – all of the models fundamentally tell the same story, even though the specific numbers and their derivation may differ. **We don't need to be stats geeks to understand the key ideas.**

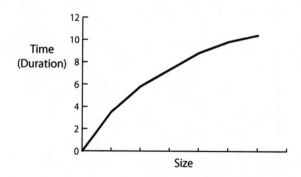

The first point common to all successful models is that they represent non-linear behavior – the fractional exponents in the formula shown above. The chart shown here illustrates the relationship between software "size" and project duration. We see that as size increases, duration also increases, but at a decreasing rate – twice as big does not mean twice as long. Many   factors, far beyond the ability of anyone to intuit, influence the shape of the curve – tools and models are absolutely essential to getting it right for all but trivial projects.

A second point common to all models is that they require some quantification of size – several methods exist, none fully satisfactory, but any method is better than none. It simply is not possible to do a professional estimate without quantifying size. Realistic estimates for software projects require quantification of size – early estimates are simply very rough guesses, not a basis for firm budgets.

Among the immature 85% size is very rarely quantified and models are almost never used. Among the 15% size is always quantified and models are always used.

Here we see the relationship between size and effort – again non-linear. As size increases so does effort, but at an *increasing* rate. Double the size always means significantly more than double the effort.

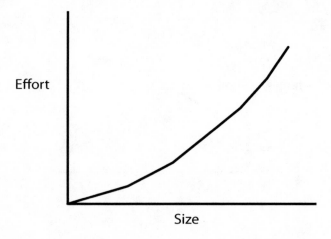

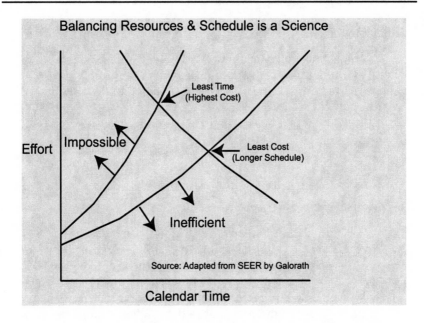

As a practical matter there are upper and lower bounds on the duration of software projects as illustrated in the graphic above, graciously provided by Dan Galorath. The upper (minimum duration) boundary is simply defined as the lowest known duration for a project of a given size developed in a stated context (technology, experience, etc.) – anything less is a 3-minute mile – there are no "existence proofs".

The "least cost" boundary reflects the limits on customer's patience – rarely does it exceed 130% of the "least time" minimum schedule – we might call the least cost boundary "improbable". This "lower right" extreme is the "cheapest" solution, while the other extreme is "fastest", but also *maximum cost*.

In between these bounds is the feasible solution space – the tradeoff between time and effort is a management choice – unfortunately the immature 85% group very seldom realize these implications and actually make a conscious, deliberate choice. Sometimes faster is really necessary, but the real cost should always be understood.

Note that this relation is entirely independent of actual productivity – different productivity and size levels are simply the same curve, shifted down and left if higher, right and up if lower. If you want it both faster AND cheaper you MUST either increase productivity - which takes time - or reduce size, often a near term option.

Planning

Three Schools of Thought

1. **"Traditionalists"**, in general, will attempt to create a plan that covers the entire project, start to finish. Plans such as these will begin by creating a "work breakdown structure" (a list of tasks, most associated with completion of some type of "work product" such as a requirements document, a user interface design, a piece of program "code", or perhaps a test plan.) Resources (staff) will be assigned to each task, and effort and duration will be estimated. Most of these plans will be presented in the form of a "Gantt Chart" as illustrated below. Although rarely done among the 85%, a few advanced practitioners may go a bit further and defined "predecessor/successor" relations among the tasks to create a "Critical Path Network" (more about that in part 3.)

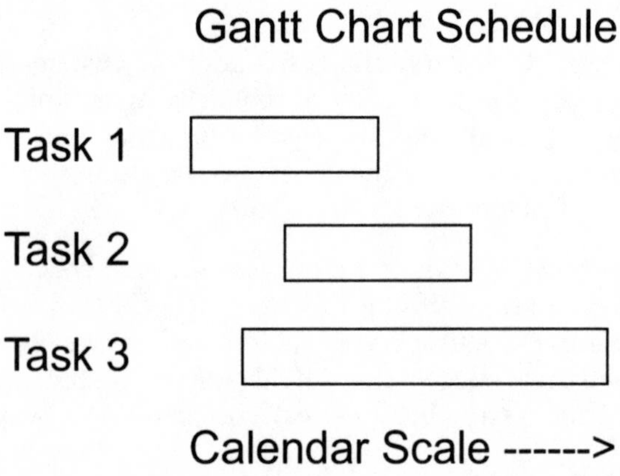

Gantt Chart Schedule

Task 1

Task 2

Task 3

Calendar Scale ------>

This sort of planning rests on the premise that requirements are or can be known. Hence planning done in keeping with this school of thought will usually plan the requirements gathering activity as one phase, and then prepare the remainder of the plan when that phase is complete or nearly so. This school of thought has been comprehensively defined and standardized by the Project Management Institute in their Project Management Body of Knowledge®.[2]

Contrarians argue that this model is fundamentally flawed because it is alleged to proceed on the assumption that requirements are "frozen" and will not change. Contrarians may also argue that in many cases customers simply don't know what they require – exploration and experimentation will be required to discover what is truly needed.

2. "Agilists", in general, operate on the assumption that requirements are not well understood and are in any case likely to evolve significantly during the project. Hence, those who follow this school of thought as regards planning (there are other aspects we will not examine here[3]) believe it is best to "eat the elephant one bite at a time". Most Agile methods (there are perhaps 6 or so common flavors[4]) expect to have a full time customer representative co-located with the software team. That individual, sometimes called the "product owner", defines the requirements, sometimes known as the product or feature backlog.

A small number of high-priority features or functions are selected from the overall backlog and are "built" in short fixed duration iterations, generally 2 to 8 weeks in duration. Each iteration is expected to deliver working software – perhaps a prototype subject to further revision based on customer feedback. Several iterations are often required to produce a product that is sufficiently complete to be deployable for actual customer use. Planning in this model is typically limited to the current iteration only, for which a task list will be created and individuals will be assigned. In this school of thought the duration of each iteration is fixed and the volume of requirements selected is whatever the team believes can be completed in that interval. In general agile methods advocate reliance on "tacit knowledge" – conversation rather than comprehensive documentation – in order to minimize overhead and waste. Contrarians argue that this approach does not scale well to larger projects for several reasons:

- Estimates tend to be limited to the current iteration, making total project budgets difficult to determine.

- Undertaking small parts in a series of iterations often means there is a lack of overall architecture. Later iterations may find it is necessary to move a load-bearing wall. Rework can become excessive.

- In some domains a lack of documentation is simply not acceptable – e.g., when compliance with FDA standards for medical devices is required, or when TL9000 compliance is mandatory.

3. "Agnostics"[5], in general, operate on the premise that the schools described above are both valid within certain contexts and are not fundamentally incompatible. They can be, and often should be, judiciously combined. Among the 85%, unfortunately, the sectarians more often than not prevail. Nuance is just too difficult, and the "standards police" frequently rule.

In practice, there is nearly always a certain degree of truth to both of these arguments. Equally, they are often overstated – certainly some changes will occur, and certainly some requirements are not fully understood. Clearly this is a spectrum with many projects occupying the middle third where the "best" choice is not entirely evident. The following hypothetical example illustrates a blended approach.

Blending Traditional and Agile Methods: An Example

Objective: Replace an obsolete legacy credit card billing system that has the following attributes:

- Large (~ 8,000 function points); probably > 800 person-months

- Most requirements are unchanged from the existing system

- Deployable only as a complete system

- Numerous complex interfaces require extensive regression testing

- Various regulatory requirements for documentation & standards adherence

- User interface needs extensive re-design, details/options not well understood

- New federal legislation/regulations will constrain interest calcs; alternatives need to be evaluated and prototyped / tested against historical data to optimize profitability

- Most testing and construction will be outsourced; requirements, top level design, high risk development elements, and acceptance testing will be in-house

Could this really be done totally Agile? Very unlikely!

Does it make sense to use traditional methods for the UI and the interest calc? Not a good option – Agile is clearly better for these elements

Among the 85% project planning is generally a serious weakness. Most of the plans we see are deficient in one or more of the particulars discussed below. Many are based on fundamental misconceptions.

- Many plans lack sufficient detail. Sound plans will be granular – tasks will be perhaps days or at most 2 weeks in duration.

- Many tasks lack clearly defined end states. Often it is not clear what "finished" really means.

- Many plans lack specific tasks to verify quality and perform rework. In organizations where a "test only" approach is the norm, any assertions about status of early tasks are invariably misleading. A design document may exist, but if it has not been checked for errors, and those errors have not been corrected, is it really "finished"?

- Many organizations utilize astonishingly complex planning and reporting systems and tools that are intended to serve many masters whose needs are often mutually contradictory. Customers want to view work in progress; they want to understand the status of the budget – how much has been spent, how much is available; they want to understand planned vs. actual effort, cost, and schedule for each project. CIOs and their direct reports want to understand how staff resources are allocated. Project managers want to know what each member of the team is working on and how that work is progressing. The quality manager (if there is one) wants to know how many defects are being found and fixed.

- Many software organizations will need several percent of total headcount just to install, maintain, and operate these systems.

Yet, in most cases, the data being collected and reported is shockingly inaccurate. Many of these systems are classic examples of "more is less". Far too much data is collected and excessive amounts of effort go into trying to understand and explain the various anomalies that arise. Many software project and departmental managers spend more time trying to explain the numbers than they do actually managing projects!

- Most organizations in the 85% group do not differentiate between time reporting and project status tracking. This fact contributes mightily to inaccuracy of both time reporting and status tracking. Certainly it is true that managing a project means defining the work to be done (the task list) and periodically checking to determine which tasks have in fact started and/or completed.

That does not mean that it is necessary to track time at the task level. Yet, in practice, most organizations do not recognize this distinction. The result is that the "chart of accounts" (list of time-charge categories) for time tracking is far larger than is actually useful, resulting in a lot of useless overhead and frustration. Time tracking at the task level is useful in a mature organization that is actually capable of using advanced methods such as the Earned Value Management System[6]. That level of time tracking is a complete waste of effort that actually detracts from effective management among the 85%.

Methods, Standards, and Tools

"Productivity" in software has been a holy grail for many years, and remains just as elusive as for Arthur's knights of old. The software industry has long been afflicted by many maladies (dragons not among them), and a great deal of effort and thought has gone into how to make it "all better". Much of that effort has not generated significant results. Nonetheless it seems useful to understand where we've been, if only to avoid searching the same ground again. The keys are not under the street light where we've been looking for years.

A Brief History of Improvement Approaches in Software and IT

A Google search (Fall 2009) on the term "software process improvement" yielded 3,520,000 hits. Quite an amazing number especially when we compare how much has been written to how little actually achieved. Clearly this is an area where there is a huge gap between "opinion" (very few facts support most of these ideas) and reality. In general, software process improvement approaches fall into two broad categories, potentially used in a vast array of combinations:

- Software related standards, including those promulgated by ISO[7], IEEE[8], the SEI[9], PMI[10], ITIL[®11] and many, many others. 58,100,000 Google hits on this topic.

- Software development methodologies, including general categories such as "waterfall", "iterative", "agile", etc. with dozens or hundreds of variants within every known category.

Clearly this astonishing array of ideas cannot be known to or understood by anyone, let alone widely shared. Equally clearly all of this effort has not resulted in anything resembling the phenomenal rate of improvement realized in hardware products such as microprocessors. Certainly it is true that software and IT projects have grown enormously in scope and complexity over the years, and also generally agreed that absent all of these tools, standards, and methods things would be far worse. Yet, delivered quality, productivity, and cycle time have not improved nearly as much as market pressures require.

Standards – "Compliance" vs. "Performance"

While not the fault of the standards themselves, and certainly not the intention of those who developed them, the operational reality of many standards-based improvement initiatives has been to institutionalize a "compliance" mentality at the expense of a "performance" focus.

Software and IT standards essentially identify relevant processes, describe desirable attributes of such processes, and in many instances provide an assessment or evaluation scheme that can be used to evaluate the "maturity" (degree of compliance with the standard) of the organization with respect to those processes. The SEI's CMMI[®12], for example, identifies 25 "process areas" and a five level maturity scale (inspired by Crosby's "Quality Maturity Grid"[13]). Originally developed for application to large defense contractors, where it is de-facto a requirement, CMMI has seen fairly wide use in the commercial sector as well, both in the US and especially in Asia. Similar standards, ISO 12207 and the companion ISO 15504, are more widely used in Europe.

Sadly, many organizations involved in CMMI (and other standards) have become overly focused on obtaining a maturity rating as a goal (a compliance focus), and have lost sight of the intent – i.e., improving performance. None of the standards currently in use connect actual performance to maturity level.

Standards are designed to focus on "what" should be done and offer little if any explicit guidance on "how" to achieve the intent of the standard. Most standards encourage measurement, but are not specific about what to measure, how to measure it, or how to use the measures to drive improvement.

Software Development Methodologies – So Many Choices, So Little Impact

A Google search on "Software Development Methodologies" (SDMs) turned up over 9 million hits in Fall 2009. SDMs address the "how" of certain IT and software processes, but typically do not concern themselves with measurements, and virtually never address process improvement. Discussions of the pros and cons of the very large number of approaches and variants strongly resemble theological discourse. Facts are conspicuously absent, anecdotes abound, and partisan fervor is abundant.

Capers Jones has identified thirty historical problems that have affected software engineering for the last fifty years, and states that none of the various methods have succeeded in solving all thirty problems.

Whatever the pros and cons of any particular method in practice, there is very wide variation between actual practice and the method or process as originally formulated. Worse, there is virtually no objective evaluation of the actual performance of any of these methods. Getting past mythology is long overdue.

Is Agile "Fragile"?

While I'm not intending to be unduly controversial (well, maybe a little), I have noticed more and more commentary recently expressing various concerns about a current "hot topic" - Agile methods. One example is a recent article by James Shore, "The Decline and Fall of Agile"[14].

In that article he remarks "It's odd to talk about the decline and fall of the agile movement, especially now that it's so popular, but I actually think the agile movement has been in decline for several years now. I've seen a shift in my business over the last few years. In the beginning, people would call me to help them introduce Agile, and I would sell them a complete package that included agile planning, cross-functional teams, and agile engineering practices. Now many people who call me already have Agile in place (they say), but they're struggling. They're having trouble meeting their iteration commitments; they're experiencing a lot of technical debt[15], and testing takes too long."

Personally I don't doubt there are many potential benefits of Agile methods, provided they are actually used as intended and are appropriate to the context in which they are applied. Sadly, like many other good ideas, Agile is often more "talk the talk" than "walk the talk". Some of Agile's more rabid advocates seem think it's a "universal solvent", which even alchemists and sorcerers don't believe any more - nothing turns lead into gold.

On the other hand, I do have some fundamental concerns about the evident lack of hard facts and data - there seems to be a lot of heat, but not much light. Are Agile methods actually more productive in aggregate across a series of iterations compared to alternative methods? As Shore points out, "technical debt" can easily become a major problem. To some extent short iterations are necessarily risky to architectural soundness. Of course Agilists advocate "refactoring" to remedy that risk, but how often is refactoring actually done? What does it actually cost? After 10 or so iterations is Agile really, in total, more productive than another alternative?

And what about test driven development ("TDD")? What does

it cost compared to formal software inspections? What are the actual defect containment rates? Capers Jones data and other sources clearly show formal software inspections find 60- 80% of the defects present while testing finds 30-50% (per test type). The facts we do have call into question some of the claims made for TDD.

In fairness, my comments about lack of facts and data are by no means restricted to Agile - they apply to a great many fads du jour. Let's hope one day soon we'll begin to do rigorous data based assessments. Sadly, though there is certainly merit in most of these highly touted concepts and tools, none of them has ever been or ever will be a universal solvent. Used in the right context many can be helpful, but they won't turn lead into gold. None of them will enable you to run a 3-minute mile any time soon!

Let's declare a moratorium – "No New Methods" – let's learn to use the ones we have. The method we use has some impact, but other issues are much more significant.

Silver Bullet Syndrome

Software tools are designed for use by people who are engaged in various aspects of software and IT including requirements, design, construction, testing, "inventory" management, etc. A Google search on this topic results in 213,000,000 hits. Many of these are aggressively marketed as "Silver Bullets". Wild claims abound – to mention just a few (these are quotes from real products whose names shall remain anonymous to protect the guilty) ...

> *"... Since these Test Cases are based on actual, documented requirements, the test team can be sure that they are testing 100% of the application's functionality"*

> *" ... the only multi-platform UNIX C/C++ programming environment that provides the interactivity you need to maximize all of the benefits of C++ and object-oriented programming"*

"… the most effective black-box, negative test solution for developers…"

"… a scalable out-of-the-box solution, at a great value …"

" … will help your business achieve CMMI 2/3 in a quarter of the time and a fifth of the cost …"

Many of these products are very new. Most have little if any supporting facts or data, but lots of cool features in the demo.

In spite of a paucity of evidence supporting the effectiveness of software tools, many software and IT professionals have a fascination with tools and an almost mystical belief that somehow the right tool will make everything better. Occasionally this is even true to some small degree. In the broad sweep, however, tools are only as good as the processes within which they are employed, and the people who use them.

For quite understandable marketing reasons, tool vendors tend to build tools that are "process independent" in order to address the broadest possible set of opportunities. Unfortunately, this means that in many instances the tools are sub-optimal with respect to any particular process, or are overly complex in their attempts to provide the flexibility to adapt to whatever process is being used.

Proliferation of tools that do essentially the same thing is rampant – for example, The Language List by Bill Kinnersley[16] lists 2500 different programming languages, some no longer used, but many still found. One of them is appropriately named "Babel". Many organizations today have dozens of programming languages in use. Excessive variety may satisfy individual tastes, but certainly does not contribute positively to efficiency and flexibility in the workforce.

"Silver Bullets" include many varieties of the very latest whiz-bang tool or concept that will sweep away all cares and woes. No doubt you've encountered silver-tongued gurus and sales types pedaling the latest form of salvation. I've been hearing these stories for more than 40 years – I've even told some of them myself before I learned better.

Many of the more important influences on productivity are actually quite mundane – perhaps that's why they get so little attention. We will discuss those in Part 3.

Product Quality

"Get mad, then get over it." - Colin Powell

Sometimes we all feel we'd like to throw the bloody computer out the window – natural enough, but not really an option. Far more constructive to understand why there are so many defects and what can be done about it. Quite often an excessive number of defects are traceable to events that occurred (or should have occurred but did not) long before the software is actually delivered. "Getting over it" means understanding the root causes and changing behaviors to ameliorate those causes.

Like it or not, developing software is a difficult task. There are many opportunities to make mistakes and preventing them, while possible, is a longer term undertaking that is in practice achieved only by the elite 15%. In the near term the focus for the 85% will necessarily be on (1) accepting the fact that a lot of mistakes are made and will be made for the foreseeable future and (2) exploiting proven methods of "appraisal"[17] to greatly increase defect containment rates.

The number of mistakes likely to be made is called "defect potential", and it grows with the size of a project. The table below gives typical numbers of potential defects, defects delivered, and containment rates[18] on a "per function point" (size) basis for several sample project sizes. As we see, the containment rate ("TCE" – total containment effectiveness) declines as size increases.

Size	Function Points	Typical Cost ($US)	Defects		
			Potential	Delivered	TCE%
Very Large	100,000	$500,000,000	950,000	240,000	75%
Large	10,000	$25,000,000	76,000	16,700	78%
Medium	1,000	$1,000,000	5,000	750	85%

Adapted from Capers Jones © 2007

Potential defects are "inserted" at each step of the process – some relate to requirements, some to design, some are found in the configuration parameters used to tailor purchased software to local needs, and some are found in the program instructions ("code") used to build custom software. More defects are found in test plans, and some defect repairs are faulty and cause (or reveal) secondary problems.

The distribution of defect origins will typically look something like the adjoining graph. More than 50% of all defects (including documentation defects) originate before "construction" (custom coding or purchased software configuration[19]) begins. Among the 85% virtually no effort is expended to find the pre-code defects until most of the construction is completed and testing begins.

More than 40% of delivered defects originated in requirements and design. Properly understood this is simply malpractice. Failing to apply proven methods of finding defects before construction is equivalent to engineering a bridge without doing stress calculations to determine the gauge and strength requirements for the steel and concrete to be used. Were software "engineers" subject to licensure equivalent to other engineering professions they would surely be found liable for widespread negligence.

Defect Origins (%)

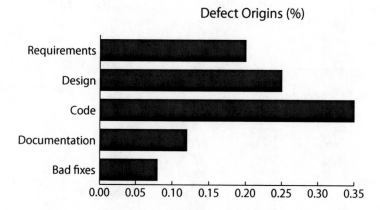

Testing is certainly necessary and no responsible person would advocate not doing it, but having said that it is also very expensive and not very efficient.

A typical "today" scenario relies entirely on testing. A series of different types of tests are used. These go by various names – "unit", "integration", "system", "acceptance", etc. Some of this testing is strictly manual; some uses software tools to achieve a degree of automation of the process. Regardless of the means used, 'traditional' test methods generally find between 30 and 50% of the defects present at the beginning of each test type. The results of this approach may look something like the following table.

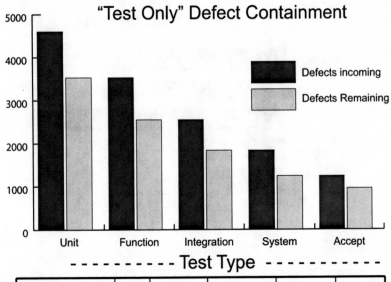

"Test Only" Defect Containment

Test Type	Unit	Function	Integration	System	Accept
Defects In	4601	3531	2546	1836	1238
Defects Found	1150	1059	764	642	310
Bad Fixes	81	74	53	45	22
Defects Remaining	3531	2546	1836	1238	950
TCE %	23.3%	44.7%	60.1%	73.1%	80.5%

This scenario illustrates why the immature 85% organizations average a total containment rate (TCE %) of around 80-85%.

In contrast, the 15% organizations will use a scenario that includes additional appraisal methods to discover and correct defects at each stage as they are introduced. In Part 3 we will examine those additional alternatives and quantify the impact they will have (hint – much better delivered quality, at lower cost).

> "...until the software industry can routinely top 95% in average defect removal efficiency levels, and hit 99% for critical software applications, it should not even pretend to be a true engineering discipline. The phrase "software engineering" without effective quality control is a hoax."
>
> – Capers Jones, Best Practices in Software Engineering McGraw Hill 2009

Measurement

"You can observe a lot just by watching." – Yogi Berra
"Measure twice, cut once" – Carpenter's mantra

Sadly, most software and IT shops measure a lot of stuff that's basically pretty useless and often don't accurately measure the things that really matter. Often a lot of confusing detail is presented that obscures more than it reveals. Averages are presented without standard deviation. Means are used when percentiles would be far more appropriate. In Part 3 we will look into what measurement data should be provided. Here we focus on the flaws in what most organizations actually have (and don't have) today.

When it comes to software projects the things that matter most are:

Effort – labor hours. Labor is by far the largest element of total software project cost. And, these labor hours are among the most expensive in the entire organization. Many software groups do (ostensibly) track effort hours and "charge back" to internal and/or external customers, yet that data is almost always very seriously inaccurate. Organizational assessments often find total hours reported for a given period are significantly less than a simple 'sanity check' would suggest. One would expect, for example, that total hours reported in a given week would at least equal 40 hours (or whatever the nominal work week is) times headcount – in practice the hours actually reported are frequently 20-40% less than we would expect! Few organizations even bother to check. Ask your internal audit group to take a look – if the data are even 90% accurate that will be a great surprise. Accurate time accounting is a basic fiduciary duty of any software organization – it's the owner's money – they have a right to know where it goes.

> **CAVEAT:** While it is certainly an obligation of every individual to accurately report time, it is equally the responsibility of management to use that data in a fair and responsible manner. As Deming and others have asserted, individual data (as opposed to aggregate process or team level data) should never be used to evaluate, reward, or punish individuals. Many factors, often un-measurable, contribute to how long it takes to perform a particular task. Software development is not like auto repair, plumbing, or wiring – every project is unique – the work required is creative and not standardized and highly repeatable – "standard hours" are fundamentally impractical and unworkable. Measures are necessary to manage and improve processes in aggregate but counter-productive when attempts are made to apply them to individuals.

When we drill down into how those hours are distributed to the various projects underway we often see even greater distortions – time is often charged to a project with remaining budget authorization, even when work is in fact devoted to a different project entirely.

The picture gets even worse when we consider the next level of detail. Software time tracking systems often attempt to collect data by project phase and within phase by task for each software project – the "chart of accounts" (list of time-charge categories) for a typical software project will include dozens or even hundreds of categories. In practice the 85% organizations almost never actually use any of this detailed data, but for some strange reason many continue to incur the overhead required to collect that data. A single individual will often be charging to a dozen or more categories in a single week. Cynicism about the value of this abounds, the accuracy of the data is abysmal, and no wonder – those reporting regard the entire effort as an exercise in futility!

When it comes to time accounting among the 85%, less is definitely more! In part 3 we will discuss what to do about this – you can get far more actionable information from far less reporting.

CAVEAT: Organizations that bill customers by the labor hour, such as outsourcing firms and government contractors, will generally account for all hours. Among the 15% organizations the internal discipline necessary to ensure accurate distribution of effort hours to phases and tasks is also often in place. The assertions above are accurate for the vast majority of the 85% organizations, including many outsourcers.

Size of the project. Size is an "independent variable" that has been shown to be an important predictor of effort and duration of software projects. Sizing a software project is a very challenging undertaking – software is inherently intangible – you can't weigh it or measure it with a micrometer or volt meter. Nonetheless a variety of approaches to sizing have been developed[20] – none fully satisfactory, each with pros and cons. Any method of sizing is better than none. Sizing is almost always done among the 15%, rarely among the 85%. Absent sizing, your building contractor will give you a price without knowing square feet, floors, windows, and doors – prospects for realism are exceedingly dim.

Defects – finding and fixing them - account for at least 40% of total software costs – the largest single element. Yet, few organizations among the 85% accurately measure the number of defects found by the various means used to find those defects. As indicated in the adjoining table, more than 40% of organizations surveyed don't measure even a narrow definition of software quality (defects)[21]. Fewer than 20% measure both defects found by testing (prior to release) and those found after release.

Quality Measures

None	44%
Customer defects only	30%
Test + Customer defects	18%
All pre- & post-release defects	8%

adapted from Capers Jones
2008 survey of 300 organizations

If available, these data allow calculation of a very basic "containment rate" – i.e., the percentage of defects found before release. Current US average containment rate is around 85% - i.e., 15% of all defects are found by customers!

Even fewer, around 8%, measure all defects found (not just those from testing). This is a critically important metric, because it is both far cheaper and far more effective to find defects before testing even begins. When these rates are measured as a project progresses they can be used to check the project's overall health and forecast the final result.

Some organizations (30% in this survey) have reasonably good data about defects found after the software is delivered – these defects are usually tracked by the help desk or support organization. A few organizations, especially those with test groups independent of the developers, do a reasonably good job of tracking defects found during testing. In those instances where the data are reasonably complete (18% in this survey) it is a simple matter to calculate the containment rate – yet, among the immature 85%, very few do so. This is really rather astonishing – comparable process defect rates (such as manufacturing yields, sales close rates, credit default rates) are virtually always evaluated in other areas of the business – why not for software?

There is an old saying in the software business – "we can deliver it really quick and really cheap if it doesn't have to work." Cynical, but containing a grain of truth. In highly competitive software market segments it is well known that some software companies focus on feature time to market and intentionally let their customers find a large share of the bugs. We all experience this phenomenon in new releases of software – we often find we must "re-boot" several times every day.

Unfortunately there are no readily available quality data on software products comparable to J.D. Power reports in the automotive sector. It certainly would be nice to know what the defect containment rates are for popular software products. Wouldn't it be refreshing if software firms decided to compete on quality rather than on obscure features most of us don't need and won't use? (Dream on!)

Unlikely you'll be able to influence the software vendors generally (unless you are one), but certainly you can change the rules of the game within your own organization. You could, in some cases, contract for quality – e.g., by specifying financial penalties based on the number of defects found after installation. Certainly you expect to receive credit for defective products received from all sorts of vendors – why not from software vendors? Sadly, some vendors (e.g., Microsoft, Intuit) have so much market power it is unlikely you will have enough leverage to influence their behaviors, but many smaller vendors will accommodate.

You could also require "quality adjusted" reporting of planned vs. actual project results. We'll discuss how to introduce quality centric metrics and controls in Part 3. As Crosby has pointed out, "Quality is Free"[22] (or at least cost-effective).

Duration seems simple enough – end date minus start date. In practice it's not so straight-forward and often impossible to determine in retrospect. Several issues arise:

- "Start" is often ambiguous – does it mean the date the project was approved? Or the date a project manager was assigned? Or the date staff was assigned and work actually began?

Frequently it is not possible to determine the meaning after the fact.

- "End" can be fuzzy as well – does it mean when development says the project is complete? When the acceptance test is passed? When the system "goes live"? We often see project data within the same organization that is based on different definitions.

- "Re-plans" – for a variety of reasons many projects are re-planned several times during execution. Estimates may (often do) turn out to be way off. Scope may have changed, re-organizations may cause projects to be placed on hold, manpower may not be available when needed, contracts may not be in place, etc.

Generally when projects are re-planned they are "re-baselined" – i.e., the old plan is discarded (or perhaps archived) and the new plan becomes the basis for monitoring going forward. More often than not the original planned start and end dates are lost. Typically the reasons for the re-planning are also difficult to determine after the fact – it's usually not clear how much the scope (size) of the project changed.

Many organizations report actual vs. planned schedule for completed projects using whatever happened to be the most recent re-baselined dates.

A "typical" re-plan scenario:

The original baseline plan indicates 12 months duration and 10 person years of effort. The re-plan happens when scope increases 10% due to certain additional requirements being introduced. The project was four months along and thought to be about 1/3 complete. The resulting new baseline indicates an overall elapsed duration of 16 months and effort of 14 person years. In total a 25% increase in duration and a 40% increase in effort – even though scope only increased 10%! At this point we often hear screams of outrage from the business client – "What?!! Why so much?"

The client is in a bind. They've already spent 1/3 of the original budget, the business need remains unmet, the new target date is still 12 months away, and the forecast cost to complete is now greater than the original budget! Not good, but in most cases the project goes forward anyway.

The software team heaves a sigh of relief. The original target date and budget were "negotiated" down their throat in the first place – they had estimated 14 months and 12 person years, but their estimate was rejected and they agreed (under pressure) to do it in 12 months with 10 person years of effort. When we look at the new baseline from their point of view the "real" increase in schedule and budget is 14% - given some rework of completed materials are required, that seems pretty reasonable.

The "truth" resides is in the eyes of the beholder.

When the time comes to issue summary reports on planned vs. actual project completions, which baseline is used? Assume for a moment that the project actually completes on the dates indicated in the re-plan, in which case the project may be reported as "on-time and on budget". If the original plan baseline is used, the project overruns schedule by 25% and effort by 40%. What do your numbers say? Are they based on consistent definitions and accurate data collection? If you are among the 85% it is most likely the reports you get are meaningless.

Many software and IT practitioners are resistant to being measured, often because they know from experience that measures can be used inappropriately to punish individuals rather than to improve processes. Accurate and useful measurement is often defeated because mangers fail to heed one of Deming's most important laws – "Drive Out Fear". Additional resistance to measurement arises because practitioners know that in most cases the data are highly inaccurate (and hence not really useful for decision making), and also because the level of detail required imposes an unreasonable overhead.

Measurement is absolutely central to any improvement strategy focused on software projects. The following table approximates the state of the industry today – where does your organization fit? We'll discuss how to move up the performance curve in Part 3.

Software Measurement Maturity	Crosby's "Quality Management Maturity", adapted to software projects				
	1:Uncertainty	2:Awakening	3:Enlightenment	4:Wisdom	5:Certainty
Management Understanding	No Comprehension of quality as a Management tool	Quality might be valuable, but not funded	Learning, becoming supportive & helpful	Participating, recognizing personal role	Quality is an essential part of effective management
Problem Handling	Fire fighting lots of yelling and blaming	Teams address critical issues quick fix bandaids, short term focus, problems recur	Corrective action focus, problems are faced openly & resolved in an orderly process	Problems are identified early all players are open to improvement	Most problems are prevented
Non-value-added % of effort	60 - 70%		50%	40%	20-30%
Pre-release Defect Containment	60 - 80%		85%	90%	95% +
% of Software Organizations (est.)	65%		20%	10%	5%

Status Reporting

Status reports are typically about as accurate as using a wet finger in the wind to determine how hard it's blowing. Maybe it's possible to differentiate between a tornado and a spring zephyr, but not much more. Often we see "percent complete" estimates, which project management professionals generally acknowledge are basically worthless.

How is that number derived? Is it the percent of the planned labor hours consumed to date? Does it indicate the calendar days consumed compared to days planned? If one of our team has spent 2 weeks working on a task estimated to take 2 months they will invariably report themselves 25% complete. But how do they know that? On what basis? Reality is that they don't know, and often don't care – it takes as long as it takes, and they really don't know how long that is until they're done.

Maybe it's based on someone's guess about how long it will take to finish, in which case the percentage equals the planned total minus the estimate to complete divided by the planned total. Is that really any better? Why would we believe the estimate to complete is any better than the original, especially when we know estimates are usually widely wrong. Any, and often all, of these methods are used within a single organization. Most of the time neither buyer nor seller has any idea what it all really means.

Many on the software team feel every day is like taking the kids on a long car trip – "are we there yet"? Asking them questions to which they do not know the answers simply breeds cynicism. What we often discover is that a project is "90% done" for months on end. During the first 2/3 of the project status reports did not reflect any meaningful effort to find and fix defects, so the intended "final 1/3" ends up being twice as long as planned – we've been kidding ourselves all along. If we are not getting "quality adjusted" status reports we do not have a realistic understanding of true status. Doing that is not rocket science. In Part 3 we'll get into how that can be accomplished by any 85% organization.

Part Two "Take-aways"

Risk Recognition

As with a visit to Las Vegas, executives need a realistic perspective on risk. Projects in the Medium ($1,000,000 - $25,000,000) and Large ($25,000,000 - $200,000,000) size categories carry high failure risk - 20-40% of them fail. If and/or when such projects are actually delivered they are likely to be highly defective and only partially complete. Many failures are due in part to inadequate engagement of key customer personnel – executive commitment to ensure adequate involvement of the most knowledgeable staff members is both painful and necessary.

Sizing and Estimating

Estimating is among the worst weaknesses in the software field. Excessive optimism and a lack of understanding of software "laws of physics" often leads to "3 minute mile" estimates. Among immature organizations the cost/schedule tradeoff is rarely a conscious decision based on facts and data. In Part 3 we will discuss how to deal with this issue.

Project Planning

Among the 85% planning is a serious weakness. Plans lack adequate detail, end states are not clearly defined and defect detection and rework activities are not explicitly planned. These failings lead to highly misleading reports of progress as supposedly completed work products contain significant numbers of defects that must be corrected later.

Many of these organizations utilize excessively complex systems for planning and reporting that often lead to very poor data quality – "less is more". Time reporting and project status tracking are both more effective and accurate when these needs are met by different processes, rather than by a single integrated process.

Methods, Standards, and Tools

Like the drunk looking for his keys under the street light "because that's where the light is", most immature software organizations are looking for salvation in the wrong place. New methods have not driven significant improvements in outcomes on high risk projects in immature organizations. Actual performance is what matters, not compliance with a particular approach. As we will see in Part 3, immature organizations can realize major gains using virtually any of the available methods and standards – as organizations approach Crosby's "level 4" choices of methods and standards become more important, but initially they are far down the priority list.

As with methods, tools are not going to turn lead into gold. They can be helpful in a stable process, but do not in themselves bring stability. Investment required to introduce and support these tools can easily consume millions of dollars. Learning curve on the bleeding edge often carries a significant penalty and can increase risk. That does not mean methods, standards, and tools have no value, but it does mean other actions are much more essential for immature organizations. Task switching, for example, far outweighs the impact of any particular method. Estimating and planning, quality management, project status tracking processes are all much more important than the methods, tools, and standards chosen.

Product Quality

Finding and fixing defects is by far the largest part of total software cost. Most immature organizations spend far more, and achieve far less, than is readily possible. Compared to an average immature organization that finds 85% of defects before delivery a mature organization finds 95% - and does so 20-30% cheaper and 10-15% faster. Finding defects before testing is key to significant improvement. Part 3 will suggest a defect containment regimen that will significantly improve defect containment and also reduce non-value-added costs. The proposed methods are implementable by any immature 85% organization.

Measurement

The "big 4" measures of software groups include effort (time), project duration, defects, and size. Of these many groups measure effort and duration, but rarely do so accurately. Many collect more detail than is actually useful, and the additional detail contributes to inaccuracy and leads to misleading status reporting. Few among the immature 85% measure size at all – a major contributor to estimating errors.

Generally inadequate measurement of defects among the 85% is the equivalent of might driving without headlights. Finding and fixing defects is the largest single cost element in nearly all software projects. Most 85% organizations rely on a "test only" strategy that increases project risk, leads to lower delivered quality, and is an important factor in project delays. Most of these organizations devote little or no effort to finding defects in requirements and design before construction begins, resulting in around 40% of all delivered defects traceable to requirements and design. In Part 3 we will examine a much more effective approach that will lead to significantly reduced costs.

Status Reporting

Many among the 85% rely on highly misleading "percent complete" estimates. Plans intending to devote 1/3 of total effort and duration to testing often find the real numbers are more like 2/3. In Part 3 we discuss how remedy these shortcomings.

---

[1] I can hear the gnashing of teeth from here. Agilists are irate. "We don't believe in signed-off requirements – they're going to change anyway." All very well for smaller projects in the low risk zone, but what about those bet your job career killer projects? Estimates are REQUIRED for large projects, and estimates can't be done until requirements are reasonably well known. "We don't know how long or how much" just won't fly.

[2] ANSI/PMI 99/001/2004 A Guide to the Project Management Body of Knowledge (PMBOK Guide) - Third Edition www.PMI.org

[3] For more particulars, see the "Agile Manifesto" http://agilemanifesto.org/

[4] e.g., Feature Driven Development (FDD), Extreme Programming (XP), Scrum, Crystal Methods, Adaptive System Development (ASD), Lean Development (LD)

[5] Those who hold the view that any ultimate reality is unknown and probably unknowable.

[6] The Earned Value Management System is defined by the ANSI/EIA-748 Standard. It is widely used in the defense industry and in large construction projects. Often used in the mature 15% software organizations.

[7] International Organization for Standardization http://www.iso.org/iso/en/ISOOnline.frontpage - this organization has published many software and IT related standards, often similar to those published by the IEEE.

[8] Institute for Electrical and Electronics Engineers http://www.ieee.org/portal/site This organization, among its many functions, is the designated US lead organization in the development of national standards for information technology and software development, as well as many other engineering related standards. As of November, 2006 40 Software Engineering standards have been approved.

[9] Software Engineering Institute http://www.sei.cmu.edu/, a unit of Carnegie Mellon University funded in part by the US Department of Defense to promote improvements and best practices in Software Engineering.

[10] Project Management Institute http://www.pmi.org/info/default.asp Authors of the Project Management Body of Knowledge; this organization certifies individuals as "Project Management Professional" (PMP). Widely, but not exclusively, applied in software and IT.

[11] Information Technology Infrastructure Library http://www.itil.co.uk/ the best practice processes promoted in ITIL® support and are supported by, the British Standards Institution's standard for IT service Management (BS15000). ITIL® (the IT Infrastructure Library) is the most widely accepted approach to IT service management in the world.

[12]Capability Maturity Model Integrated® http://www.sei.cmu.edu/cmmi/

[13]Quality Is Free: The Art of Making Quality Certain, by Philip Crosby, McGraw-Hill Companies (January 1, 1979)

[14]http://jamesshore.com/Blog/The-Decline-and-Fall-of-Agile.html

[15]The term "technical debt" refers to the level of disorder or lack of tidiness that tends to creep into software as it is evolved and changed. The software becomes more complex, convoluted, and difficult to understand unless continuous efforts are made to clean it up – those efforts are known as "refactoring".

[16]http://people.ku.edu) In contrast, according to http://www.ethnologue.com/, there are 6,912 known living languages in the world, which suffice for nearly 7 billion people, a ratio of around 1,000,000 individuals per language. With perhaps 5-6 million software developers worldwide the ratio is roughly 2,000 programmers per language, although the distribution is highly skewed. At this rate we can expect more programming languages than programmers within a few years.

[17]A general term that includes any and all methods of finding defects – potentially far more than testing.

[18]"TCE %" – total containment effectiveness – the % of defects present that are removed before delivery.

[19]Very little data about defect rates related to purchased ("package") software deployments is available. The defect rates may well be lower than for custom code, but it remains true that many deployment challenges occur. Budget and schedule overruns are common among large package deployments. A significant number of outright failures have also occurred, although it is likely the fail rates are lower than for custom development.

[20]The most commonly used include "Function Points" (ISO/IEC Standard 20926:2003), and "lines of code" (see Technical Report CMU/SEI-92-TR-020). Many others that are far less standardized and defined, such as "Story Points" are also used but are less common.

[21]Software quality has been defined in several ways, including "fitness for purpose", "conformance to requirements", in terms of "-ilities such as reliability, maintainability, etc.", and simply in terms of a narrow definition "absence of defects". Here we will use the more restricted definition, "defects" – anything that is important enough to fix, whether related to fitness, requirements, -ilities, or malfunction.

[22]Quality is Free Philip Crosby, Mentor 1980 ISBN-10: 0451621298

Part Three

Part Three
What You Can Do
About It
(Five Redeeming Virtues)

Book XVII, Chapter VI in the Analects of Confucius.

Tsze-chang asked Confucius about perfect virtue.

Confucius said, 'To be able to practice five things everywhere under heaven constitutes perfect virtue.'

He begged to ask what they were, and was told,

'Gravity, generosity of soul, sincerity, earnestness, and kindness. If you are grave, you will not be treated with disrespect. If you are generous, you will win all. If you are sincere, people will repose trust in you. If you are earnest, you will accomplish much. If you are kind, this will enable you to employ the services of others.' - *Translation from James Legge (in the public domain)*

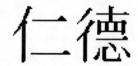

www.wearyourchinesename.com

"If you always do what you always did, you always get what you always got." - (Anon)

Introduction to Part Three

"What You Can Do About It"

Now that we have an understanding of what often goes wrong and why, it's time to consider what can be done to reduce risk and improve outcomes.

Chevy Chase once did a Saturday Night Live skit on "How to become a millionaire" – as I recall, the formula was "first, you get a million dollars ..." To put your mind at ease, what I suggest here will not cost anything near a million dollars. Modest investments, well chosen, will generate near term net savings. You won't need hundreds of consultants, a marvelous new method, or a spiffy new set of tools. Lest you feel too much at ease it's only fair to mention you will need common sense, courage in the face of adversity, persistence, and political savvy.

In this Introduction I will first provide a quick overview of the contents of Part 3 (The Five Redeeming Virtues), and then we'll review some Broader Considerations before we get into the Virtues. Here's how the topics in Part 3 fit together:

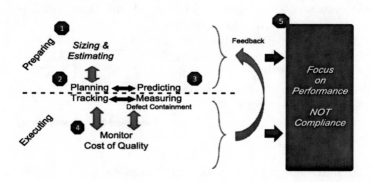

The Five Redeeming Virtues

In the immediately following section we discuss **Rationalizing Sizing and Estimating**. An Executive Summary provides a brief overview. We then consider related Roles and Responsibilities, survey Estimating Methods, describe Data Collection and Effectiveness Metrics, and review Implementation Considerations.

We then consider **Professionalizing Planning and Tracking**. Following a brief Executive Summary we discuss Roles and Responsibilities and provide an overview of the Critical Path Method, an industrial strength approach to planning high risk projects. We then review tracking methods, including the Earned Value Management system and a simpler variant I call Earned Value "lite". Suggested Data Collection is discussed and we then review Implementation Considerations, including the "Project Office". Implications for outsource situations are then considered.

The third section deals with **Predicting and Measuring Defect Containment**. Following a brief Executive Summary we explore Predicting Defect Insertion. We then examine Appraisal Methods used to find defects. Roles and Responsibilities are reviewed, and Data Collection requirements are described. Both Effectiveness and Efficiency Metrics are explored and several Defect Econometric Models are introduced. These models may be accessed from the companion web site. This section concludes with a discussion of Implementation Considerations.

In the fourth section of this Part we explore **Measuring Cost of Quality**. I provide an Executive summary and then discuss Roles and Responsibilities. Implementation Considerations are examined, including a suggested "chart of accounts".

In section five of Part 3, **Focus on Performance, not Compliance,** we discuss "Management by Fact" including an overview of the Lean Six Sigma approach to process improvement as it applies to high risk software projects. We discuss a summary Dashboard.

The book's **Conclusion** summarizes key aspects of the recommendations I offer.

No matter how well one prepares, success will not follow unless my recommendations on defects are followed. Indeed, there is a feedback loop – first class planning needs the data that comes from effective defect practices. This is not to say that better preparing actions should be deferred until defects are under control – in the preparing phase sizing and estimating are especially critical and most will need to outsource that initially - the defect actions are necessarily all internal to the group doing development.

In Part 3 I will often speak in the first person singular as the suggestions I make here are my own and do not necessarily reflect a consensus view among the cognoscenti. Some may regard elements of my advice as *heresy*. However, "we" are still in this together, so I will continue to speak at times in that mode.

We are also going to get more specific because you will necessarily need to rely on software professionals to act on these recommendations – hence I have developed a companion web site that provides another level of detail your technology partners will find useful. They will need a bit more detail than you do, so I walk a fine line in Part 3 - general managers may find some of the details hard going.

If you are a general manager and find the detail is too much in places you may wish to focus on the Executive Summary at the beginning and the "Take-Aways" at the end of the first four of the five redeeming virtues. Perhaps you will elect to scan the rest if you find it's more that you want. I suggest you read all of the fifth redeeming virtue. You need not master the details, but you will find it useful to understand some of the specifics about where this is headed so you may find it useful to scan some of the detail in each section. The benefits of my recommendations will be realized only if you set expectations and follow through. The more you understand the more likely it is you will get the results you seek. Executives managing software professionals should read all of Part three.

Broader Considerations

Following the recommendations in this book necessarily means undertaking a significant organizational change initiative. I'll not attempt to address all of the implications of that, but I believe there are a number of particularly important aspects you will need to think through early on.

Insourced or Outsourced?

Confronted with a need to undertake a large business critical software project, whether custom-built or purchase package, many organizations will elect to outsource to one of the major systems integrators. I'll not get into the pros and cons of outsourcing here, except to say that the issues covered and advice given apply equally to outsource suppliers. Claims to the contrary, the available evidence does not indicate outsourcers achieve dramatically better results than in-house projects – a bit better, not dramatically better.

It is likely to be challenging to ensure outsourcers follow the advice given here, but if you are determined you can build in contract requirements to ensure they follow best practices. Outsourcing success is more likely when customers screen and approve key team members rather than simply buying the resume of the firm. As you might expect, most of these firms will resist. We'll discuss adapting the advice herein to outsourcers at the end of the section on Planning and Tracking.

Getting Started

Today's reality in most of those organizations is a pervasive state of denial – the three monkeys (hear no – see no – speak no evil) are in charge.

Many of these organizations never get any better simply because they are not honest with themselves about

current reality. In situations like these there is simply no substitute for high level executive intervention – "do what you always did, get what you always got". Step 1 is obvious, but not simple to execute – CHANGE THE RULES.

Software Measurement Maturity	Crosby's "Quality Management Maturity", adapted to software projects				
	1:Uncertainty	2:Awakening	3:Enlightenment	4:Wisdom	5:Certainty
Management Understanding	No Comprehension of quality as a Management tool	Quality might be valuable, but not funded	Learning, becoming supportive & helpful	Participating, recognizing personal role	Quality is an essential part of effective management
Problem Handling	Fire fighting lots of yelling and blaming	Teams address critical issues quick fix bandaids, short term focus, problems recur	Corrective action focus, problems are faced openly & resolved in an orderly process	Problems are identified early all players are open to improvement	Most problems are prevented
Non-value-added % of effort	60 - 70%		50%	40%	20-30%
Pre-release Defect Containment	60 - 80%		85%	90%	95% +
% of Software Organizations (est.)	65%		20%	10%	5%

For organizations at Crosby's levels 1 and 2 (discussed in Part 2 in the Measurement section) the major challenge is attitudinal and cultural.

Take advantage of a crisis – at levels 1 and 2 they come along frequently. When there is lots of yelling and screaming and the witch hunt is about to start is a good time to strike. A pervasive norm in organizations such as these is "blaming".

> *"those IT guys never listen"*
> *"the users keep changing their minds and demanding the impossible".*

Declare a cease fire – give everybody several get-out-of-jail-free cards, but attach a few conditions. Get out of jail free cards mean there will be a strict moratorium on blaming and exiles to the gulag for a reasonable period of time provided all involved agree to full cooperation in an independent baseline assessment designed to evaluate the organization (not just the software and IT folks) in relation to the issues identified in Part 2. For many level 1 and 2 organizations this is a profound culture change – it simply won't happen without strong and sustained leadership from on high.

Often an improvement initiative will begin with an independent assessment requiring several days to several weeks of interviews and review of any data that may be available. Most level 1 and 2 organizations will need external professional assistance to do a reliable assessment. Once an organization reaches level 3 much of the capability needed to improve further will exist within the internal organization – additional help may be needed, but only selectively and short term to address well defined issues. When level 4 is reached an organization is well on its way to joining the elite 15%.

Before we get into specific redeeming virtues we will need to consider a set of broader over-arching considerations. We will need to establish an overall framework and strategy for our improvement initiative. To do that we address the following questions:

1. What precipitating events are motivating a need to improve? What do we intend to do, and why? To whom will we communicate our intent?

2. What is our overall strategy for improvement? What actions come first, what will be done concurrently? Which "sins" are causing the most pain? Often that is a difficult question to answer, because there are many interactions among the issues raised in Part 2. We will likely need to address more than one area of concern, but setting priorities that acknowledge limits on our capacity is a necessity.

3. How will responsibility and accountability be allocated? Who will be responsible for what actions? How will specific goals, targets and time frames be established? How will progress be measured?

4. Beware "initiative contention" – you may need to stop some initiatives in order to start others. More than three or so concurrent initiatives are typically a formula for failure. Do a few things well rather than many poorly.

Creating or Leveraging Motivation to Improve

Motivation always precedes change. Most of us really don't want to change – it's hard - it's painful – it may be risky. If you believe the issues we have discussed so far are relevant to your organization the essential first step is to clarify and build consensus around why a change is necessary.

In many cases the motivating event is a recent (perhaps current) "project disaster". The pain is evident to everyone. Perhaps a large mission critical project is very late and substantially over budget. Perhaps there has been a major failure that resulted in cancellation of a significant initiative and a multi-million dollar write-off. In many immature organizations such a situation leads to a witch hunt – heads roll and nothing is learned. The stage is set for another large failure in the future.

Crisis creates a golden opportunity to "unfreeze" the current state, always a necessary first step in any meaningful change process. Never waste a good crisis.

Whether or not you have an immediate crisis at hand it is generally advisable to begin the process of change with an independent and unbiased assessment. Assessments are always tailored to fit a particular circumstance.

Effective assessments will be performed by one or more very senior individuals possessing deep knowledge of software processes and best practices. Assessments must always ensure complete confidentiality for individuals – findings are fairly and openly presented, but individual sources are never revealed.

In virtually all immature organizations the findings from the assessment will themselves provide motivation for change. Assessments will give some insight into prioritization of potential actions, and will also provide a sense of the level of resistance and/ or support for change that exists in various segments of the organization. It is common, for example, to find significant differences between executives, managers, and workers as well as between business customers and software/IT professionals.

Formulating Strategy

It is most likely that an assessment will reveal a need to improve in most, perhaps all, of the deadly sin areas discussed in Part 2. So where do you start? Certainly not an easy question and one that has many possible answers. For many organizations strategic priorities will likely be set as follows:

*   Assign first priority to actions that improve control of high risk projects in order to reduce probability of outright failure and reduce cost and schedule overruns. In order to achieve that objective an organization must:

*   Require professional, independent "should cost" estimates for all high risk projects. This topic is examined in the section entitled **Rationalize Sizing and Estimating**.

*   Ensure Planning and Tracking processes produce plans that are sufficiently granular and include specific tasks and resources for appraisal and rework activities in each phase of the project. Require Critical Path planning for all high risk projects. Insist upon Earned Value 'lite' status reporting. We consider how to do this in the section titled **Professionalize Planning and Tracking**.

*   Apply an appropriate level of effort, using appropriate appraisal methods, throughout the software development or package deployment process. Specific methods and suggested level of resource allocation are discussed in the section titled **Predict and Measure Defect Containment**. If you do not currently know your defect containment rate, which is very likely, action in this area will certainly have more leverage and result in quicker payoff than any other actions you may take.

*   Assign second priority to implementation of the Cost of Quality framework. This will most likely require significant changes to existing time accounting systems and related processes such as chargeback where that is being used. This is likely to meet with significant resistance, as it will reveal the true state of the emperor's attire. If you don't do this you will never know how much of your expenditures are value-added. Without that in-

formation you will never know whether or not the other actions you have taken were effective.

Many organizations will undertake this initiative in parallel with priority 1 actions. It is likely you will need 6 to 12 months to implement valid cost of quality measurement. During that time other actions you take as priority 1 will already be producing benefits. The section titled **Monitor Cost of Quality** goes into "what" and "how".

- Assign third priority to a fundamental change in the culture to **Focus on Performance, not Compliance**. This means making "management by fact" a day to day reality. Easy to say, not easy to do. In this section we will explore another pragmatic adaptation of a proven set of ideas – Lean Six Sigma 'lite'. As with many other ideas, 80% of the benefit comes from 20% of the substance. You don't need to drink the entire pitcher of Kool-Aid.

As Pfeffer and Sutton point out, "One important reason we discovered for the knowing-doing gap is that companies over-estimate the importance of the tangible, specific, programmatic aspects of what competitors, for instance, do, and under-estimate the importance of underlying philosophy that guides what they do and why they do it." Lean Six Sigma embodies a guiding philosophy.

Allocating Responsibility and Accountability

I suggest you give serious consideration to appointing a "Chief Measurement Officer" (CMO) or equivalent reporting to a sufficiently high level in the organization to ensure independence and objectivity. Ideally this person is Lean Six Sigma literate, but at a minimum this individual must have both depth and breadth in software process and metrics issues. This responsibility should not be assigned to anyone within or directly accountable for performance of the development organization, whether internal or outsourced.

The "CMO" must take care to facilitate, not dictate, all details of necessary measurement systems related to Cost of Quality and Defect Tracking. In the end, however, someone needs to own the data and ensure it is accurately reported and acted upon. This function could be one of the responsibilities of a "Project Office". Upcoming sections in Part 3 get into specifics.

Task Switching

Most software team members are frequently forced to shift from one task to another, often several times in a single day. This a very destructive practice – "task-switching" leads to many needless errors, and is inherently inefficient. A recent article in the New York Times[1] reported "... researchers at Stanford University published a study showing that the most persistent multitaskers perform badly in a variety of tasks. They don't focus as well as non-multitaskers. They're more distractible. They're weaker at shifting from one task to another and at organizing information. They are, as a matter of fact, worse at multitasking than people who don't ordinarily multitask."

Developing software is inherently complex – many facts need to be kept in conscious memory – deep concentration is a necessity. Ding! The phone rings. It's some trivial question that could easily wait, but all that complexity so painstakingly assembled in conscious memory is gone in a flash. Ten or twenty or thirty minutes later we've finally gotten back to where we were when the phone rang, and the project manager drops by – "are we there yet?" No wonder many programmers wear ipod headsets – it's not to listen to the music, it's just a bit of white noise to surpress interruptions.

Interruptions can be (but usually aren't) managed. Doing that will have far more impact than the choice of a methodology or standard. Once a week is often enough to find out if we're there yet. On critical projects make sure you have dedicated teams and interruptions are minimized.

Specialization

Another root cause of many software issues is traceable to a lack of specialization. Estimating is a good case in point. Most estimates are developed by project managers in collaboration with their teams. A typical large project manager prepares an estimate perhaps once per year, and devotes a very small percentage of time to that activity. Hardly surprising most do not become adept. As we will explore when we discuss each of the redeeming virtues, I believe there are a number of areas where specialization is essential. Most immature organizations do not have the necessary range of specialized expertise in house today.

You will need external help, but in most cases you should insist that any external assistance you acquire includes a requirement to train and mentor carefully chosen internal resources to take over from the consultants within a reasonable period of time. In some instances it may make sense to enter into longer term outsourcing agreements if the volume of specialized skill required does not justify permanent internal resources. Large project estimating may be such an instance in organizations that are not doing a substantial volume of high risk projects – the need for special expertise may be sporadic and impractical to maintain internally.

Irrespective of how you elect to staff the required specialized expertise – insourced or outsourced – it is essential that these individual's responsibilities and accountability is carefully distinguished from those of the teams who actually do the software development or configuration work. Teams themselves must remain fully in control of planning and defect containment. More about this as we discuss each virtue.

OK – enough context – let's get to specifics.

Rationalize Sizing and Estimating

Executive Summary

Software project estimating is a serious weakness among most of the 85% organizations as evidenced by the large overruns of both cost and schedule documented by the Standish Group reports mentioned earlier. When estimates are unreasonable many serious consequences ensue.

This section discusses what must be done to improve in this critical area. Briefly, having an effective sizing and estimating process means:

- Making a very early determination if a proposed project is in the high risk zone. If it is, extraordinary steps are required. Even some projects not in the high risk zone in terms of size may merit extra precautions if failure has potentially serious consequences. "First approximation" sizing is important, but should be understood to be very preliminary – not a basis for firm budgets or schedules.

- Serious estimates necessarily depend on an adequate understanding of the actual requirements – vague hand waving is not enough. Requirements must be sufficiently well understood to enable quantification of "size" using a metric such as "function points". The software team must know required business rules, inputs, outputs, data sets. That will mean committing a serious amount of time from your best people. Expect requirements identification to cost 7 – 10% of the total project budget. Serious planning of large projects cannot realistically start until requirements are known. Review what is being requested and prune non-essentials.

- Two fundamentally different estimating methods are applicable to large projects – "top-down" and "bottom-up". High risk projects should *always* use both methods as cross-checks against one another. In general the "top-down" estimate should be prepared by an independent party as a sanity check against estimates prepared "bottom-up" by the development team using the Critical Path Method (described in the next section on Planning and Tracking).

- *Never* commit to going ahead with a project until all planning guidelines discussed in the section on *Planning and Tracking* have been satisfied – i.e., a detailed plan has been prepared and reconciled to the independent top-down estimate. An out-of-control project is one that does not have time to plan. Rush now, pay a lot later.

- *Never* negotiate schedules. A professional estimating process will provide the best estimate obtainable – if you can't afford it, don't start. Don't kid yourself – the 3-minute mile is not going to happen on your watch.

- Hold teams accountable for quality first, schedule a distant second.

First Approximation

"Triage" comes first – is the magnitude of a project you are considering large enough to be in the high risk category? As we have seen in the risk recognition section of Part 2, projects in the "medium" and "large" categories have 20-40% failure probability. This is a trip to Las Vegas, and it's time to decide how much you can afford to lose – if it's over the threshold you will need to take extra precautions before committing yourself.

Step 1, therefore, is to determine at least approximately how big this project is likely to be. If it's in the medium or large category the advice provided in Part 3 is entirely applicable – if it's not you can apply business as usual processes without undue risk.

Until requirements are well defined there will necessarily be a degree of uncertainty about how large the project actually is, but it is nearly always possible to get a "quick size" first approximation.

Most commonly one of two approaches are used, and sometimes both. The first approach develops an approximate count of "function points" and the second develops an approximation by analogy – i.e., we identify "similar" projects and base our first approximation on what they actually cost to complete. You may have the capacity to do this initial approximation in house and you can easily find external sources to do so. Often it is best to get several opinions to get a sense of the range of uncertainty – expect significant variance across multiple sources. Take into account vested interest and potential bias of those providing the estimates.

"Function Points" are one of the more common methods used to quantify the size of a software product. Unfortunately, they have been labor intensive and hence expensive for larger projects. Recent developments are beginning to significantly reduce effort and cost – an October 2009 paper on new approaches may be downloaded from: http://www.isbsg.org/isbsgnew.nsf/WebPages/EDA63BCD863ED3DFCA25749E001F101D/$file/Function%20Point%20Business%20Model%20CAPERS%20JONE%202009.pdf

If the project under consideration falls into the high risk category it is critically important that requirements are defined in sufficient detail to enable realistic planning of the remainder of the project. In practice this means all stakeholders must be identified and interviewed (possibly at some length) to enumerate all required data, all interfaces to other systems, all inputs, all outputs, and all queries. Business rules and workflow requirements must be described. You must provide adequate access to your best, most knowledgeable staff – shortcut this at your peril.

Requirements Definition

As a rough order of magnitude you can expect determination of requirements will consume 7 – 10% of total expected project cost. If, for example, your first approximation estimate suggests you are going to spend $10,000,000 you may reasonably expect defining requirements will cost roughly $700,000 to $1,000,000. Think of that as your ante to get a seat at the table. Don't commit to spend anything more until you know a lot more about the stakes and the odds. Don't be completely surprised if it turns out the real size of your project is significantly greater than the first approximation. Be prepared to take a hard look at what is "required" – prune non-essentials.

The requirements gathering phase should be planned in

accordance with the guidelines provided in the next section on Project Planning and Tracking.

Determining requirements can turn into "analysis paralysis". Requirements may be inextricably interwoven with business process reengineering. There are no easy answers to that dilemma, but for our purposes here the key thought is that we must know what the real magnitude of the requirements are before we commit to going any further.

Many projects are doomed to fail from the start because they commit to execution prematurely. Teams start executing while re-engineering decisions are still being made. Many changes result – lots of rework – lots of waste. Please, aim before firing. Patience is a virtue. Until we know what "it" is we cannot know how long it will take or what it will cost.

I am not suggesting that it is necessary to be obsessive about getting every detail about the requirements. For example, it is not necessary to determine exactly which data elements are required in each input or output – we do not need user interface layouts or report formats to understand requirements. As Einstein said, "as simple as possible, but no simpler."

Neither am I suggesting a requirements process need necessarily be monolithic. If the problem at hand can usefully be partitioned into smaller independent units, by all means do so. If the problem is amenable to an Agile approach, by all means use it to reduce cycle time. Unfortunately, many larger projects are to a significant extent monolithic.

Sizing

In most areas of business activity there are well understood and readily measured definitions of "output" – a ton of steel, a thousand invoices, 200 patient visits, etc. What is the comparable measure of output for software?

We cannot have a meaningful discussion of efficiency or productivity without some agreed metric of output – cost per ton, revenue per patient day, or whatever.

One of the special challenges of the software field is that output is fundamentally intangible – it is the embodiment of business rules, formulas, decision logic and data in the form of a "program". It cannot be weighed or measured in any physical sense and we cannot determine voltage or any other attribute that directly corresponds to provable laws of physics.

Yet, the fact remains that if we are to measure and consequently manage software productivity, we must have an agreed measure of output. All responses to this problem to date rely on what are known as "proxy"[2] measures – there are a variety of proxy measures, including "function points"[3], "lines of code"[4], and many, many others. These and other size measures have been shown to be statistically correlated to effort, schedule duration, and delivered quality – in other words, while they do not directly measure the size of the software, they in some degree facilitate measurement of productivity.

I do not advocate measuring software productivity per se. There are a great many reasons for variation. In practice productivity will vary across application domains, as a function of size, from project to project, and as a consequence of many factors often difficult to quantify. Rather, I believe it is much less complicated and more generally useful to focus on value-added effort as an aggregate indicator of "productivity". Value-added is independent of factors that lead to variation in productivity. I doubt there will ever be any single number that provides a meaningful gauge of "productivity" in the usual cost per unit sense across software projects.

Virtually all proxy metrics of size will work in certain circumstances and fail in others – there is no single "right" answer. The arcane details of this topic are beyond the scope of this book, but a take-away for all readers is quite simple – without sizing, all software estimates are equivalent to night driving without headlights! Any conversation about productivity in software is meaningless without an agreed measure of size.

The acid test of whether or not you have "enough" understanding of requirements is whether or not an experienced estimating professional can determine the "size" of the requirements. Most often that means estimating the number of "function points". In some instances other sizing methods may be used, but we need not go into that here. Few of the immature 85% will have the in-house expertise to reliably determine size. Even if you do it's not a bad idea to get a second opinion – if they vary significantly, explore the reasons for the differences. Doing so will clarify matters that will otherwise come back to haunt you later.

Estimating Methods

Three methods are in common use. The first method uses "rules of thumb" that are reasonably adequate only for very small projects – using these on large projects is malpractice.

The second method employs a "top-down" algorithmic approach. Given size and other parameters related to team experience, methods to be used, tools, and other factors these models provide an estimate of total effort and duration for the project, a distribution of that effort across project phases (e.g., design, construction, test), and an uncertainty band (typically +/- one standard deviation) around the estimate. This is the method most likely to be used by an independent estimator. Any proposal from either in-house or outsource suppliers that is outside the uncertainty range provided by this method should be rejected unless supported by verifiable facts and data. Estimates outside the +/- one standard deviation range are generally not plausible.

The third method also employs an estimating tool, but one that is based on activity based costing. Rather than an algorithm that estimates total effort and duration for the project, this approach produces estimates at the activity or task level and sums them to arrive at a total. This method is more commonly used in conjunction with a "bottom up" estimate in which a detailed work breakdown structure is developed as described in the upcoming section on Planning.

"Top-down" and "bottom-up" are used as cross-checks on one another. Given the same assumptions they will generally produce very similar estimates. Assumptions are explored when significant differences result from the different methods. We parse "assume" – ass-u-me. Unrecognized and often incorrect assumptions are the root of many evils.

The tools used to support methods two and three are also able to accommodate an estimate of "requirements creep" – i.e., the expected rate of growth in requirements over the duration of the project. Experience generally suggests requirements (size) will grow at a rate of 1-2% per month. Controlling this rate of growth is a management responsibility – strict approval processes are a necessity, especially later in a project. Late changes can cause major rework to previously completed elements – please, don't move load-bearing walls. Before approving any change ensure a careful assessment of the impact – and include time in the plan to do that.

Estimates are not a once and done activity – whenever there are significant changes in project scope or requirements they should be revisited. Estimates should also be updated at each phase end tollgate.

Using "Top-down" and "Bottom-up" Estimates

Once the experts agree that enough information about requirements is available to give a confident estimate of size it is then possible to use one of the commercial estimating models to develop what may be called a "top-down" estimate for the complete project. To get best results and to ensure objectivity it is best to retain an independent expert to prepare a "should cost" estimate. This estimate is in addition to those prepared by the in-house team and/or by outsource suppliers. The independent top-down estimate is used as a sanity check against the other estimates. Expect them to differ. Explore the differences – doing so will clarify matters that are going to surface later anyway.

Estimates supplied by the software team(s), whether in house or not, should be based on detailed "bottom up" project plans. Provide sufficient time and information for prospective suppliers to do a thorough planning job. Make no commitments until you have detailed plans that meet all of the criteria discussed in the upcoming section on Planning and Tracking.

Commitment Tollgate # 1

When plans have been "sanity tested" and independent experts agree plans for the remainder of the project are realistic and attainable you are ready to commit to the next phase of the project. Or perhaps decide it's really not worth what it will cost.

Roles and Responsibilities

Estimating is best done by specialists. If your software organization is large you may be able to justify that expertise in-house, but if not, outsource that role. There are a small number of firms, most of them suppliers of estimating tools, who are top notch experts. ALWAYS get an estimate from an independent party not responsible for the software project itself. Especially in the instance of outsourced development (but also in-house) there are mighty incentives in play that will tempt the developer to "low-ball" the estimate – these big projects are great resume builders for the developers and lucrative to outsource firms as well. Outsourcers are very skilled at the change-order game and will recover any shortfall later in the project.

Independent estimates are used to evaluate the credibility of estimates or bid proposals from the development team(s). If a prospective developer proposes a 3-minute mile that fact will be revealed by the independent estimate. In rare cases developer claims may actually be defensible – however, extra-ordinary claims require extra-ordinary evidence.

Data Collection

Many estimating tools provide a mechanism to collect actual values as they occur. Whether or not kept within the tool it is highly desirable to keep a comprehensive 'log' of all estimates – date, size at that date, estimated effort and duration per phase at that date, actual effort and duration to that date, and a narrative discussion of any changes in assumptions that occurred since the prior estimate. This "journal" will aid estimating specialists in refining their craft and making appropriate adjustments to reflect peculiarities of the local environment.

Effectiveness Metrics

Measuring estimating effectiveness is very straight forward – (estimated) / (actual) – perfect estimates are 1.0, low estimates are < 1, high are >1. The same formula applies to both effort and duration estimates. The effectiveness indices must be re-determined whenever size changes, or alternately adjusted to reflect those changes. When estimate vs. actual varies by more than perhaps 10% a postmortem should be conducted to identify opportunities to improve future estimates. Don't expect to get closer than +/- 10%.

Implementation Considerations

Select an independent estimating expert with the clear understanding that they are not eligible to bid on any project for which they produce an estimate. If you intend to have an in-house team develop the system under consideration they should also use an estimating tool, usually one based on activity based costing. They may also need to retain an estimating expert to help them use the tool effectively. In the best case the outside expert will use a top-down approach and the internal team will use bottom-up. Hold the selected team responsible for:

- Creating and following a "bottom-up" plan that is reasonable vis-à-vis the independent "top-down" estimate

- Creating and following a plan that is consistent with the guidelines provided in the upcoming Planning section

- Quality of the delivered product consistent with the upcoming section on Defect Containment. If you outsource INSIST on a delivered quality guarantee – it's worth paying a bit of a premium if you must.

- DO NOT evaluate internal teams on actual vs. estimate, but DO hold them accountable for delivered quality. If you follow the approach I propose the estimate you get will be the best obtainable. It may or may not be correct, but it's the best money can buy. If you outsource you may be able to negotiate a fixed-price agreement, but beware the change-order game.

No matter how much you dislike the estimate you get, NEVER override it – as Colin Powell famously said, "you break it, you own it." If you are dealing with an outsource arrangement it certainly makes sense to negotiate the price, but not the proposed level of effort or calendar duration.

Sizing and Estimating "Take-aways"

"Triage" always comes first – you are off on a trip to Las Vegas – think through your risk tolerance – find out how much is likely to be at stake.

First approximations are just that – expect the initial estimate to change significantly. Make sure those doing sizing are up on the latest approaches – sizing is critically important, but don't spend more than necessary.

Realistic "bottom up" plans cannot be developed until requirements are reasonably well understood – don't stint on involving key staff if you want to get it right – pay now, or pay a lot more later. Don't commit beyond requirements until you have a solid bottom up plan.

Get independent "should cost" estimates developed using "top down" methods. Make sure assumptions are explored and bottom up estimates converge with top down. Don't commit to the next phase until independent estimates have been sanity checked and reconciled to estimates prepared by the development team.

Make certain estimates are developed using adequate expertise and tools appropriate to the task. This is not the place to rely on amateurs.

Hold development teams accountable for quality as a primary consideration. Don't focus on schedule. Ultimately you'll get it sooner and at lower cost if teams are evaluated on quality first.

Professionalize Planning and Tracking

Executive Summary: Planning

One valid definition of an "out of control" project is one that doesn't have time to plan – large projects should expect to devote ~5% of total effort to planning and status tracking. Planning and tracking adequate for high risk projects requires a significant level of effort that leads to a granular plan. These plans will consist of short tasks, most no more than one week in duration.

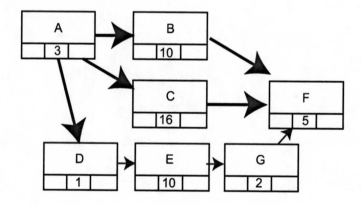

Plans adequate for high risk projects will always use the "Critical Path Method." Critical Path Method is an industrial strength project planning technique that defines dependencies among tasks (called predecessor-successor relationships). This method is supported by industrial strength tools that, among other things, allow us to accomplish "resource leveling" – i.e., to ensure we have not committed someone to spend more hours than are available within a certain time period. No 80 hour weeks.

Under the "Planning Methods" heading below we will discuss the how-to of this method, but for now a case in point illustrates how important it is.

Several years ago I was retained by the risk management committee of a Fortune 100 company to help management evaluate a major software project (a purchased package implementation) that had twice been rescheduled and was millions of dollars over the original budget. Management had lost confidence in the estimates and status reports they were being given.

To make a long story short, I found a 200 person project being managed with 12 separate plans that involved shared resources across the 12 sub-teams. There was no visibility into the impact of resource sharing, as with 12 plans it was not possible to aggregate individual commitments across plans. When consolidated to a single plan we found some individuals were scheduled 90 hours in a week! Many other deficiencies in the existing plans were also evident.

To remedy the deficiencies and get a realistic schedule and budget we initiated a 3-month critical path planning exercise that developed very detailed "bottom up" lists of tasks, resources assigned, and inter-task dependencies – in all 10,000 tasks. The result was a credible schedule and budget that exceeded the original estimates by 9 months and millions of dollars. The project was cancelled at a saving of about $10,000,000 (as against a cost of planning of ~ $1,000,000)

Had executive management been aware of the importance of professional planning, a major write-off could have been avoided by adequate risk management at the outset.

Roles and Responsibilities

This case contains several key lessons that are universally applicable to all high risk projects:

- To the maximum extent possible it is always desirable to involve those who will actually do the work in the planning process. Few will feel committed to estimates made on their behalf by others. A common failing in project planning occurs when project managers or others go off and make a plan without involving those who will do the work. Mid-level managers often feel they "know better" and may override task level estimates made by teams – this rarely turns out well. When I review plans I will often ask those assigned (privately) if they are comfortable with the estimates for tasks to which they are assigned. Squirming is a bad sign.

- It is always necessary to have a single plan, all within a single file in a single planning tool. In the case cited above the team had 12 different plans – in part because they were using MS Project and were finding it could not effectively accommodate the volume of tasks across the entire project. The tail was wagging the dog. High risk projects need industrial strength tools. Building a 10,000 task plan meant first acquiring an industrial strength tool that was up to the challenge.

- No one among the 200 individuals assigned to this project had ever undertaken a planning effort of this magnitude – they simply did not know how to start. Professional project planning facilitation is critically necessary for high risk projects. Most project managers in the immature 85% organizations rarely if ever undertake high risk projects successfully. Make certain you have a planning facilitator who has "been there and done that" – most likely you will need an outside resource. That outside resource should be expected to train and mentor your team to institutionalize this critical capability.

Executive Summary: Status Tracking

Among the 85% status tracking is also a serious weakness. Most projects provide highly optimistic reports during the first half or two-thirds of a project, only to see the picture turn grim later on.

Mature organizations use an industrial strength method known as the "Earned Value Management System", which is defined by an ANSI standard. In practice this is beyond the capability of most in the 85% group, but they can use a simplified approach I call "Earned Value lite". Both are described in this section. Neither relies on "percent complete" as an indicator of progress, as most project management professionals agree that is a flawed metric that tends to be misleading.

This section also discusses the concept of a "Project Office" – an approach often used to effectively manage project planning and tracking and in some instances estimating, sizing, and measurement and reporting of defect containment and cost of quality. Implications for outsource situations are also discussed.

The Critical Path Planning Method

Critical Path Method is an industrial strength project planning technique that should ALWAYS be used for every project in the high risk category. Critical Path Planning begins with a "work breakdown structure" (WBS) – a detailed hierarchically organized list of tasks. The top level of the hierarchy is the "phase" of the project (e.g., Requirements, Design, Construction, Test, and Deploy) – phase names will vary as a function of the particular methodology in use. The phase level will be successively decomposed into smaller steps until tasks at the lowest level are on the order of one week in duration.

Obviously it's not a trivial task to produce such a list for any relatively large project, but if your team can't make the list they certainly can't forecast a reliable completion date either.

Given the WBS, the next step is to define who will work on each task, how much effort (hours, days, or whatever) each resource will devote, and what the overall duration (calendar time) will be. To make reasonably accurate estimates the tasks will need to be broken down into small steps, usually 1 to 2 weeks in duration. This level of detail is critically important because estimates of shorter tasks tend to be more accurate, and also because short tasks facilitate accurate status reporting.

Tasks are assigned to specific individuals (if known) or to "generic" resource categories such as "analyst" or "programmer". Each lowest level task must have a clearly defined deliverable or end state so as to ensure no ambiguity about the meaning of "finished". Preferably each task is assigned to one person and there are no concurrent assignments. Task switching should be minimized.

Next, the predecessor/successor relationships among the tasks are defined. This will define what can be done in parallel and what must be done in a pre-determined sequence – i.e., a description of dependencies among the project tasks, but also external dependencies. All of this information is entered into one of the Project Management tools such as Microsoft Project (adequate for smaller projects with a few hundred tasks) or for larger projects (thousands of tasks) you will need an industrial strength tool such as Artemis or Primavera.

Note that a 50-person team working for one year means something like 2500 one-week tasks. Given all of the aforementioned data, these systems will be able to calculate early and late start and finish dates for all tasks, the "critical path", and the amount of slack available on each task.

A very simplified critical path network looks something like the one below. Arrows indicate predecessor / successor relationships – i.e., B cannot start until A is completed, F cannot start until B, C, and G are completed, etc.

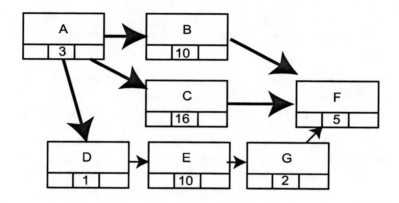

Duration of each task is indicated below the letter identifying the task – hence the software can calculate path durations as follows:

ABF – 18 days   ACF – 24 days   ADEF – 22 days   ADEGF – 24 days

ACF and ADEGF are "critical path" – any delay in these tasks will change the end date of the project. On the other hand, ABF (specifically B) has 6 days of "slack" – we can delay the start or completion of B up to 6 days without any impact on the end date. Understanding of what is and is not critical facilitates resource allocation as obstacles arise.

Sounds like a lot of work - actually, it is a lot of work - definitely not something you want to require unless you really need to know the status of your project as you go along.

Appraisal tasks must be explicitly planned and in aggregate represent a reasonable allocation of effort adequate to ensure defect containment consistent with targets. These activities and associated metrics are discussed more fully in the upcoming section on defect containment. If plans do not include adequate allocation of effort for these activities in the early phases the inevitable result will be a longer than planned test cycle. Detailed suggestions for how to plan and schedule these activities will be found on the companion web site.

Plans should also include an explicit allocation of time to evaluate the impact of proposed changes in requirements as the project progresses. In general 1-2% of total effort will be sufficient. In large projects the absence of stringent change control can lead to significant growth in the size of the project that in turn often leads to significant rework. Do not allow changes to be made casually without careful evaluation of the impact those changes will have – often what seems simple on the surface has significant implications.

Project plans should also include specific allowance for project management time – in general around 5% of total effort is reasonable.

Software teams undertaking large projects may assert, often legitimately, that they do not know enough early in the project to prepare a complete plan reflecting the level of detail I have suggested. Large projects will often use a "rolling wave" approach to planning in which the current phase is planned at the level of detail I suggest and later phases at a more summary level. This is a legitimate option, but you should always insist on details for the current phase. Never give the go-ahead for the next phase until you have a detailed plan that meets the criteria I have outlined. If your team claims they cannot provide details it is very likely they also cannot successfully complete the project in the time frame proposed. If they know how to do it, they also know how to plan it.

Tracking Methods

The Earned Value Management System (EVMS - an ANSI standard), is used by mature organizations for project status tracking. Using EVMS requires a mature Project Management process and a Project Management Office. Virtually none of the 85% organizations can realistically apply this method. However, there is a feasible alternative that delivers much of the benefit – we will look at that shortly.

Even though most of the 85% won't be able to use EVMS right away, it is nonetheless useful to understand the key ideas. To over-simplify somewhat, "earned value" is simply the ratio of the time (or cost) it did take to complete all of the tasks actually completed up to a particular point in time ("time now"), compared to the time (or cost) we planned for those tasks to take. Notice this method is conservative – no "partial credit" is given for tasks started but not completed – "% complete" estimates are not used with this method. So long as tasks are short this has little consequence.

For example, suppose we planned to complete 10 tasks, each 10 hours of effort, at a rate of 1 per day for a total of 100 hours over 10 days duration. Suppose we have completed 2 of 3 tasks we had expected to complete as of "time now" (day 3) as follows:

Task	BCWS	ACWP	BCWP
1	10 hours	8 hours	10 hours
2	10 hours	15 hours	10 hours
3	10 hours	12 (incomplete)	0
Total	30 hours	35 hours	20 hours

- BCWS: Budgeted cost of work scheduled (planned value)

- ACWP: Actual cost of work performed (actual value)

- BCWP: Budgeted cost of work performed (earned value)

The next diagram provides an example of one way to portray this information.

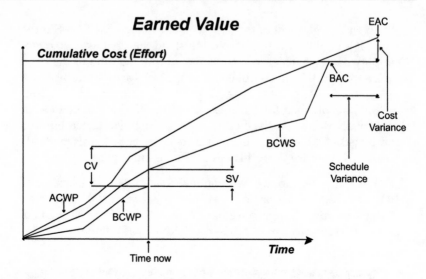

You will notice a set of abbreviations on the chart – here are the definitions along with the associated values based on our simple example above:

- BAC: Budget at completion = 100 hours

- EAC: Estimate at completion = BAC / CPI = 100 / .57 = 175 (75% overrun!)

- SV: Schedule variance = BCWP – BCWS = 20 – 30 = -10

- CV: Cost variance = BCWP – ACWP (positive is favorable) = 20 – 35 = -15

- SV% = SV / BCWS = -10 / 30 = -33%

- CV% = CV / BCWP = -15 / 20 = -75%

- CPI: Cost Performance Index = BCWP / ACWP = 20/35 = .57

- SPI: Schedule Performance Index = BCWP / BCWS = 20/30 = .67

Earned Value shows us how our actual rate of development ("productivity") compares to the rate that was assumed when we prepared our estimates. In this illustration it's a pretty dismal picture – we're 75% over budget and 33% behind schedule as of "time now". Clearly it's time to take a serious look at what's going on – maybe our estimates are bad or maybe there is a "special cause", but in any case some action is probably indicated.

Virtually none of the 85% organizations can realistically apply this method today. It requires a level of discipline and process maturity that most simply do not have. You must have accurate task level time tracking to use the full EVMS. However, there is a feasible alternative, I call it "earned value lite", that delivers much of the benefit.

Earned Value "Lite"

Earned Value "lite" requires a reasonably detailed project plan that includes expected start and finish dates for each task, but does not specifically require either critical path or full-blown EVMS. Many 85% organizations can do this. It does not require task level time tracking, but it does require objective monitoring of tasks planned to start and end vs. tasks actually started and ended.

The chart on the top shows planned (darker bar) and actual (lighter bar) starts, while the one below is planned and actual finishes against a timeline, updated at "time now" (day 3 in this example) to reflect actual status of tasks. Data used here is the same as the EVMS example above.

Together these charts give a very clear picture of real status – when the light and dark bars diverge they clearly indicate whether the project is ahead or behind.

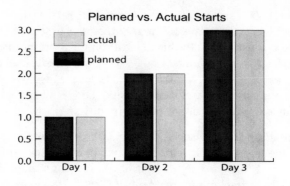

Planned vs. Actual Starts

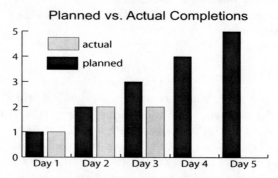

Planned vs. Actual Completions

EV "Lite" makes several important simplifying assumptions:

- ACWP = total effort charged to the project as of time now. In our example, as of day 3, 35 hours have been charged to the project in total.

- We do not attempt to track actual time at the task level. i.e., BCWS = the sum of the estimated effort planned for those tasks planned to be completed as of time now.

- If a task is late the actual effort expended is assumed to be proportionate to the ratio of tasks that were scheduled to be completed / the number actually completed. i.e., BCWP = BCWS * (# tasks actually completed / # tasks scheduled to complete)

Example: BCWP = 30 * (2/3) = 20 – the same result we get from the more formal method provided the simplifying assumptions are in fact valid. Most of the time they are very close.

Clear and unambiguous definitions of what "finished" means for each task are a critical ingredient. Ideally completion status is independently determined by someone not directly responsible for project performance – i.e., a fair and objective observer.

Data Collection

The data we require include:

- A count of tasks planned to start and finish each week – we get that from our project plan

- The total effort we planned to expend for tasks planned to start and finish respectively – we sum the estimates included in our plan to obtain this number. Virtually any project management tool will enable us to easily execute a query to obtain this value.

- Total effort expended on the project as of "time now". Typically that value will be taken from your Cost of Quality time tracking system. Alternately, if you elect to track time at the task level in your project management system the value comes from that.

Implementation Considerations

When it comes to estimating, project planning and tracking, defect containment, and measurement there is simply no substitute for independent, objective, and expert opinion. I believe that every organization undertaking high risk projects needs to establish a focal point for these efforts. In many organizations this takes the form of a "Project Office". The role of the Project Office is analogous to that of a Controller – not doing the project work, but advising on best practices and reporting objectively on actual results.

To be effective this entity needs to report to a sufficiently high level in the organization to ensure total independence and free access to all necessary information and expertise. At a minimum the Project Office must have a full time employee (not a contractor) directing this function. Depending on the volume and frequency of high risk projects that individual may have a full time staff or may contract for various specialized skills on an as-required basis.

The concept of a "Project Office" has been applied successfully in the Construction and Defense industries for many years as a tool to manage risk on major projects. In these days of out-sourcing and business process transformation, the Project Office can help you manage the business risk inherent in any significant change initiative. While the examples discussed here deal with exceptionally large-scale situations, the key ideas apply to any important initiative where you face "bet your job" risks. Whenever you're doing something that "can't be allowed to fail" the Project Office provides valuable insurance.

When the Project Office May Be Used

Scenario 1 - "We must transform our business in order to survive. To survive, we must reduce our cost base by at least $ 1,000,000,000 over the next three years. To achieve this we will reduce our work force by 8%, which will be enabled by integrating and extending our existing information systems infrastructure."

There are dozens of large companies that fit this description today. Perhaps yours is one of them. In many organizations the ability to implement necessary systems and re-engineer business processes is an important obstacle to success. This is a situation tailor-made for use of the Project Office.

Scenario 2 - "Due to the increased competitiveness in our industry, our earnings per share growth has slowed and our stock is now under-valued. To increase shareholder value we must improve our margins, which we plan to do by consolidating our redundant and incompatible divisional information systems into a single common system. This strategy is expected to save at least $100,000,000 over five years."

This is another very common occurrence in today's environment. Pulling this off probably means selecting an integrated application software package and perhaps engaging a consulting firm. How does a firm that has never undertaken anything even a faction the size of this effort avoid being at the mercy of suppliers that stand to benefit from over-runs and delays? An effective Project Office can provide the expertise and objectivity needed to help the company manage the consultants and package vendors.

Scenario 3 - "In order to reduce unit costs and increase our access to scarce technical resources, we have outsourced our internal IT function to a major systems integrator. The integrator is committed to improve productivity, reduce unit costs and deliver the same volume of software we have developed in prior years."

We read of deals like this nearly every week. But what is the definition of "the same volume of software" or "productivity"? How will that be measured, and by whom? Clearly both parties may have a vested interest in shaping the answers to their own advantage. A Project Office staffed with measurement expertise can provide a means to assure a fair balance of interests.

Why the Project Office is Used

First and foremost, the exclusive focus of the Project Office is on Projects. The Project Office is not responsible for product to be delivered by the project; rather it is responsible for ensuring that every reasonable step is taken to ensure the success of the Project. This is a crucial distinction. The effective Project Office is structured to insure independence and objectivity. Its principal objectives are, first, to facilitate open, fact-based dialog between customer and developer regarding the processes to be used to maximize chances for success and second, to provide objective and independent assessments of estimates and status.

Developers (bless them!) tend to become very focused on the products (systems) they are developing and quite naturally are less interested in abstractions such as "process" or mundane details such as estimates (trust us, we'll get it done).

Customers (bless them too!) have a tendency to be focused on the demands of the shareholders and on the deadlines forced on them by competition. They may be equally disinterested in "process" and often feel vulnerable when they must rely on technical staffs whose pronunciations are difficult to understand and more difficult to evaluate. Small wonder they may impose deadlines, attainable or not, since they (and perhaps the developers as well) have no way to know what is realistic (just get it done, whatever it takes).

This gap in perceptions is often fatal, since many large projects fail! Many of these failures may be traced to unrealistic expectations and unrealistic estimates. In my consulting practice I often see project schedules that reflect rates of delivery that are 50% greater than the project team has ever delivered in the past!

Project Office to the rescue! Very senior people whose in-depth knowledge of the processes required to make large projects succeed staff the effective Project Office. They know how to evaluate the reasonableness of project schedules, and they have expertise in the estimating process itself. They understand project planning (critical path method), definition of deliverables, the role of quality assurance, how (and when) to construct an effective test plan, how to measure and monitor progress and status and how to manage "scope creep".

The Project Office staff, because their careers are not dependent on those who manage the project, is free to speak up when insiders may not be able to take the political risk. If the project team has not made reasonable allowances for quality assurance effort and related rework the Project Office will attempt to negotiate a workable plan, or, failing to do so will "go public".

Because Project Office staff is not responsible for business operations, they are free to point out that the customer is imposing unrealistic deadlines or has failed to establish clear and stable requirements. Projects are most likely to succeed when the legitimate interests and needs of both customer and developer are balanced. The Project Office provides a mechanism to facilitate and promote true partnership.

How to Establish the Project Office

1. Make sure that the Project Office contains the expertise needed to ensure success. At a minimum, the Project Office must include at least one senior individual with large-scale project management experience. The combination of expertise required will depend on the specifics of the project portfolio and on the capabilities and experience of developers and customers. At a minimum, expertise in estimating, quality assurance processes, project management and facilitation are essential.

2. Make sure the Project Office is independent and objective. Typically this means that the Project Office will report to a level in the organization that insures free access to key people and the opportunity to escalate critical issues to the highest levels. If either the customer or the developer can silence the voice of the Project Office its effectiveness is compromised. To ensure objectivity one clearly does not place the fox in with the chickens. Beware the contractor who insists on providing the Project Office and resists oversight by outside experts.

3. Make sure that staff members of the Project Office approach their task with a positive outlook. The Project Office is not an audit function. It is not an enforcement mechanism. The purpose of the Project Office is to bring industry best practices to the fore and to do everything possible to encourage their use. The Project Office has an obligation to speak candidly based on experience, to encourage and persuade, to facilitate and to make visible. In the end, the project team and the customer must decide and act. The Project Office succeeds by forming alliances around the idea of a win - win for all concerned.

4. Recognize that the Project Office is intended to ensure that the right things are identified and done - by someone qualified to do them. This does not mean that all of the functions mentioned here (and many others not discussed) are actually done by Project Office staff. Specific expertise, such as estimating or test process assessment, may be contracted or borrowed from

elsewhere in the organization as and when required. The key role is to ensure that the right activities are in the plan, and that they are in fact executed to the agreed standard.

Functions of the Project Office

The functions performed by the Project Office may vary significantly to suit the specific circumstances and also change as the project moves through its life-cycle phases, which typically include **scoping, source selection, detailed planning, monitoring, and wrap-up/post-mortem.**

During the scoping phase the PO may be asked to assist the customer in defining the scope and boundaries of the project(s) needed to achieve a particular business objective, such as upgrading a portfolio of information systems to enable staff reductions designed to increase competitiveness in a newly de-regulated industry.

If, for example, an organization needs to reduce headcount within a three-year period in order to meet cost targets it must rapidly identify all of the systems to be developed and/or modified. Early determination of the boundaries of each project, together with preliminary "should cost" estimates, are essential to recognize the overall resource requirements.

Estimates must not be made pre-maturely - sufficient knowledge of requirements to permit sizing is an essential pre-requisite to any realistic estimate. These high level resource requirements need to be quickly translated into an acquisition strategy - what will be done in-house, what can be purchased, what can be contracted. If the organization needs 12 - 18 months to accomplish this first step (a common time frame), it seems highly unlikely that the three-year target will be met.

A key function of the PO may be to help the client to address this issue, i.e., how to reduce a 12 month scoping effort to perhaps 6 months. The PO may suggest a "massively parallel" approach with several concurrent mini-projects using facilitated rapid requirements techniques within 3 - 6 month "time boxes". These efforts may be undertaken using in-house resources (if available) or by specialized contractors.

Once adequate scope definition has been accomplished, attention may shift to the source selection phase and definition/execution of an outsourcing process if such a process is not already in place. This will require identification of potential sources, preparation and delivery of background materials for potential contractors, development of a ranking and scoring approach for contractor proposals, and preparation and/or review of contract documents (possibly including incentive and/or penalty provisions). The extent to which the PO participates in these activities depends on in-house capability and experience. Most organizations undertaking exceptionally large efforts do not have all of the necessary capability and capacity in-house.

The PO may be asked to perform independent assessments of supplier organizations (in-house or contractor) to evaluate capability/maturity of development contractor processes and practices. Such assessments may include creation or review of baseline metrics relating to historical rates of delivery, defect rates, etc. These baseline metrics are essential to evaluation of proposed schedules - if the developer has never delivered at the rate proposed, why would we believe that is attainable?

During the detailed planning phase the PO may be asked to facilitate the creation of a detailed project plan using the critical path method (essential to success in any large project). This may include training participants in the basics of the CPM approach. Failure of many large projects may be traced to inadequate planning and evaluation of alternatives. The PO acts to restrain the natural tendency to "fire" before "aiming".

Key functions of the PO in this phase include advocacy and awareness of most common and most serious project risks, acquisition and execution best practices, inclusion of appropriate quantity and type of quality assurance activity, provision for rework and integration of appropriate metrics to aid project monitoring.

The project-monitoring phase may find the PO responsible for maintenance of the CPM network and the preparation of status updates for the customer and/or the provider. The PO may perform or participate in periodic independent assessment of estimates; product quality and detailed plans (such as test plans). Typically such reviews focus more on process issues and metrics than on content, which is necessarily the responsibility of the project team.

The most important role of the PO during this phase is to ensure timely and accurate representation of project progress, risks and quality. Best practices in this area include preparation of a "Project Control Panel" to display, succinctly, key indicators of project health.

The PO's role during the **wrap-up** or **post-mortem** phase may include capture and documentation of best practices and lessons learned. Typically this phase will include collection and archiving of project metrics, such as effort months, defect rates, product sizing, tools and techniques utilized (with benefit ratings), etc.

In certain cases, such as the roll-out of a common system or other technology infrastructure across divisions, the methodology and experience of the first implementation may be packaged for repetition across sites, hopefully leading to lower risk and shorter cycle times for subsequent waves of implementation.

Key competencies of the PO include:

- Experience in large-scale project management - the PO must have the "gray hair" gained from a range of comparable efforts.

- Metrics fluency - the successful PO will understand the state of the art in project metrics and will be experienced in the application of metrics to project management issues.

- Industry best practice awareness - the successful PO knows what works (and what doesn't). Specific expertise in key process areas (such as requirements definition, systems design, inspections, testing, etc.) will be needed, but may not be full time within the team - these resources may be contracted or temporarily drawn from existing resources.

- Communications skills and diplomacy - the effective PO can facilitate real communication under potentially hostile circumstances.

Literally hundreds of scenarios exist which could effectively employ the Project Office concept to increase chances for success in major initiatives. The common factor in all of them is a rapid move to a "new level" for both the customer and the IT organization - "going where we've never gone before". A small group of high-powered helpers who have been there before can save lots of grief!

Implications for Outsourcing

If you are planning to outsource software development or implementation of a purchased software package it is critically important that you set clear and comprehensive expectations of suppliers. I suggest you include some version of the following requirements in any request for proposals. Expect push-back and resistance. Many outsourcers will prefer to provide far less information.

Suggested Proposal Requirements

1. We (the customer) require all suppliers to comply with our code of ethics. We expect and require complete openness and honesty in all of our dealings with suppliers. This includes your assurance that all required facts and data you provide in response to this request for proposal and in any subsequent contracted effort are accurate and complete. False or misleading data are grounds for termination of our relationship and may result in financial penalties. Where values of data are uncertain the probable range of uncertainty is to be indicated.

2. You are required to prepare detailed plans and estimates for each phase of the subject project. We expect and require a work breakdown structure and plan prepared in accordance with the Critical Path Method. We require specific and unambiguous definition of each deliverable item or end state associated with

each task in the plan. Our panel of experts will review your plan in detail. We may require certain changes.

3. Plans must include explicit tasks for appraisal and rework in each phase of the project. You are required to provide estimates of the number of defects expected to be "inserted" and the number of defects you expect to find and correct within each phase of the project. You are required to indicate what appraisal methods you plan to utilize. Actual values are required to be reported on a weekly basis.

4. Your plans and estimates are subject to independent review and analysis by our panel of experts. We will prepare or secure independent estimates of cost and duration and will use those estimates as a basis for good faith discussions and "reality testing" of both your estimates and ours. A contract will be awarded when and if our estimates and yours converge to an acceptable degree.

5. You are required to propose a method of sizing (e.g., Function Points) the volume of work requested and you will provide your initial estimate of size. You will be expected to evaluate the impact of any and all change requests in terms of their impact on size, effort, and project duration. No change shall be acted upon until approved in writing by our change control board.

6. You are required to provide actual effort, number of tasks started, number of tasks completed, actual appraisal effort, actual rework effort, and actual number of major defects found and fixed on a weekly basis. All completed work products are to be provided for our review.

7. You are required to maintain detailed tracking of defects. All defect records are subject to our review at any time.

8. You are required to propose a guarantee of delivered quality in the form of a maximum number of major defects to be found within three months after "go live". You will be required to fix any defects above the guaranteed number at your own expense in accordance with a service level to be negotiated.

Planning and Tracking "Take-aways"

- Expect to spend about 5% of total project effort on project planning and tracking – an "out of control" project is one that does not have time to plan.

- Always require plans developed using the Critical Path Method. Require a detailed Work Breakdown Structure that identifies "small" tasks – generally most should be no more than one week in duration. Require explicit planning for Appraisal and Rework tasks that are in aggregate reasonable in relation to industry benchmarks or locally documented past experience.

- Plan for growth in requirements over the project – generally 1% of total size per project month. Make sure proposed changes are carefully controlled through a rigorous approval process that includes careful assessment of impact.

- Require at least "Earned value lite" to track project status.

- Establish an independent "Project Office" function to monitor and objectively report status. Never allow the fox in with the chickens – always ensure the Project Office is independent of the development team.

- Set high standards for outsource providers. Require detailed information, metrics, and honesty in reporting. Specify penalties for misleading or incomplete information.

Predict and Measure Defect Containment

Executive Summary

To increase value-add the single most important thing any software organization can do is to apply an appropriate amount of resource, using appropriate appraisal methods, at every stage of every significant software project. Relying on testing alone is not a formula for success. In order to gauge the effectiveness of appraisals every software project must count all defects discovered by each appraisal. That count, together with an estimate of the number of defects likely to be present, allows computation of an "appraisal containment rate" – an essential leading indicator of project success.

A typical low-maturity software project will often find 75% or less of the defects present – in other words, 25% of the defects "inserted" will be found by customers after the software is delivered. Fixing those defects can require an additional 50% of the original project budget, but those costs are frequently invisible – they usually show up in a different line item cost category and are not traceable to the original project. These "hidden" costs of poor quality may be up to 30% of total software costs.

In this section I describe the various appraisal methods, suggest roles and responsibilities, discuss necessary data collection, describe appropriate efficiency and effectiveness metrics, and provide several "econometric" models to facilitate defect containment planning and control. These models clearly demonstrate the amazing leverage that comes from improved defect containment methods. In the last portion of this section I address implementation considerations.

In this section I have defined a set of efficiency and effectiveness metrics. General Managers should understand and require these metrics of every software team. Briefly these metrics include "Total Containment Effectiveness" (TCE) to quantify the percentage of defects removed prior to delivery of the software product, and a series of "Appraisal Containment Effectiveness" (ACE) percentages that measure the effectiveness of each different appraisal step. ACE's in total determine TCE. Efficiency metrics focus on the percentage of total effort that is "non-value-added" (NVA).

I also review the different types of appraisal methods – it's not important for General Managers to get into specifics, but it is important to be aware there are a number of methods in addition to testing and to be sure your team is using an effective mix as demonstrated by the econometric models.

Executives are highly unlikely to get involved in building the econometric models – that's a role for the software professionals. However, it is important you understand why these models are needed and what you should expect to see as a result of their development. Building the models themselves is a bit involved, but the basic ideas are not complicated. The basic concepts are as follows:

1. These models are essentially "simulations" that predict the consequences of alternative defect containment strategies. They predict both delivered quality and total non-value-added effort (cost). Effectively, these models are another level of planning and are used as an additional cross-check against the "bottom–up" plan prepared by the project team – a multi-dimensional view. I suggest you ask to see these predictions and also require periodic updates, at least at the end of each development phase. **Defect containment rates are reliable leading indicators.**

2. These models require an estimate (prediction) of the number of defects likely to be "inserted" at each stage of the development process. Most of the 85% organizations will initially rely on industry benchmarks as it is unlikely local data exist. Predicting defects, which most of the 85% never do, has several beneficial consequences:

- It focuses the development team's attention on defects, which account for the largest share of total development cost.

- It enables early monitoring of the relationship between defects likely to be present and those actually found – it provides early awareness.

3. These models also require an estimate of the effectiveness of each planned appraisal method – i.e., an estimate of the percentage of defects present likely to be found. Again, most will initially rely on industry benchmarks.

4. The models calculate an estimate of the level of effort needed to execute the volume of appraisal necessary to find the number of defects we forecast to remove. In other words, the model is a 'sanity check' on the planned level of appraisal effort – i.e., is it actually plausible to remove an acceptable volume of defects with the level of effort planned?

5. The models predict the impact on test effort that results when "pre-test" appraisal methods (described below) are used – always the best way to reduce total non-value-added cost.

6. Finally the model provides an overall forecast of both delivered quality and total non-value-added costs for any given scenario based on the parameters entered into the model. In most cases the team will model several alternatives (as I have done in the body of this section) and choose the one that delivers the best balance of quality and cost. **Many will be surprised to find the lowest cost and highest quality actually coincide – it's always "win-win" when quality comes first.**

7. These models forecast both "pre-release" (before delivery) and "post-release" (after delivery) non-value-added (NVA) effort. Test-only strategies often lead to post-release NVA equal to or

greater than pre-release NVA. When delivered quality is poor, post-release defect repair costs can be 50% of the original project budget.

Some will argue these models are not worthwhile because the parameters they require are subject to significant variation and uncertainty. While significant variation is indeed a fact of life that does not in any way invalidate the value of these models – with appropriate basic statistical methods, discussed on the companion web site, we can reach valid conclusions in the face of variability.

Just in case you get bogged down in the details, here's the bottom line:

> If the recommendations in this book are followed and the defect containment models provided are used a typical software team can reduce Non-Value-Added by 40% and reduce the number of defects delivered to customers ("TCE") by more than 70%. Scout's honor – this is not speculation.

Predicting Defect Insertion

Very few (if any) of the immature 85% will have the facts and data necessary to reliably predict the rate at which defects are typically "inserted". Most of these organizations will necessarily rely initially on industry benchmarks such as those published by Capers Jones.

If the recommendations offered here are followed, these organizations will be able, in a relatively short time, to make predictions based on locally gathered facts and data. Organizations that have locally derived facts and data will understand likely variation. Organizations with solid facts and data about defect potentials and actual containment rates are well on the way to maturity – risks will go down, value-add will go up.

Without predictions of potential defects present it is not possible to determine, until well after the fact, probable containment rates. Containment rate estimates are an essential leading indicator and an effective predictor of likely outcomes. Absent containment rates we are night driving without headlights.

Appraisal Methods

Reviews and Inspections

Let's begin this discussion with an important distinction that is not well understood within the software industry. That distinction relates to the difference between a "review" and a "formal inspection". Unfortunately these terms are used loosely and largely interchangeably when they are in fact distinctly different processes with entirely different purposes.

In practice "reviews" have no formally defined rules as to who attends, what their respective roles are to be, what data is to be collected, scope of material to be covered, or rate of review. In general, reviews cover a broad scope of material, and involve many different people from different levels and specialties in the organization. Reviews are generally quite open-ended in terms of purpose – they often explore options, discuss pros and cons, and often produce or lead to decisions about what is to be done or how it is to be approached. Requirements and design reviews are typical examples – they decide what is in and what is out, and perhaps make choices among options. Reviews will certainly find some defects, but that is not their primary purpose. Reviews are about deciding "the right thing to do".

Formal software inspections, on the other hand, have very specific rules and standards that govern who participates, what their roles are, what data is to be collected, and what scope of material and rate of review are expected. Formal inspections are totally single minded – their sole purpose is to find and fix defects. Very extensive industry experience clearly demonstrates formal inspections are far more effective and efficient than ANY other form of appraisal. Formal inspections are used by virtually all of the mature 15% on virtually all projects. They are rarely used, and even more rarely properly executed, among the immature 85%. This single practice is the most important single process change and should be implemented very early in any improvement initiative.

Formal inspection can be learned in a two-day training class and will prove immediately effective – most groups find surprising numbers of major defects during training workshops. Inspections are meticulous, labor intensive, and time consuming. Many software managers and some practitioners, in spite of overwhelming evidence to the contrary, believe that inspections are "too expensive" – "we don't have time for that". This notion is absolutely false!

Formal inspections are applicable to any and all software "work products" – requirements documents, design materials, package software configuration parameters, program instructions ("code"), test plans, user documentation, etc. Both reviews and inspections are necessary and appropriate – reviews first to decide "what" should be done, then inspections to ensure the "what" is done correctly.

It is beyond our scope here to go any further into the details of these methods, but the bibliography includes several references, including IEEE Standard 1028-2008 referenced earlier, that provide specifics.

One important aside – many quality specialists with backgrounds in manufacturing will be immediately dismissive of any suggestion to use inspections, as it is generally accepted in manufacturing circles that they are not appropriate. While true in manufacturing, the notion that inspections should not be used in software is patently false – simply put, inspections are the best option currently available to improve software outcomes.

"Static Analysis" Tools

Another option in the appraisal arsenal is called "static analysis". These are software tools that "read" and analyze software "source code" (instructions that tell the computer what to do). These tools are able to find certain technical defects very quickly and inexpensively. They work only with a limited set of code "languages" – they are not applicable to requirements or design – so they are only useful after construction is largely complete. Nonetheless, in certain environments with very large volumes of code, they are a useful form of appraisal. Most of the 15% use these tools, few among the 85% do.

"Combinatorial" Test Design

This is a relatively new approach to software test planning and design that has not as yet gained significant penetration in the software industry, but will no doubt rapidly grow in popularity as the advantages are significant.

This approach to test design is based on a statistical method known as "Design of Experiments" that has long been used in the pharmaceutical industry and elsewhere to gain a maximum of information from a minimum of "experiments". As this notion applies to software testing it means maximizing the number of defects found in relation to the number of test cases created.

The central idea is to use a tool-based approach to test planning that automatically generates a set of "test cases" that exercise combinations of values of the various input parameters relevant to a particular software product. Experience and theoretical analysis both confirm that this approach will find more defects in total compared to "traditional" (manual) test case design, and will do so at something less than half of the cost in terms of defects found per hour of test effort.

An August 2009 article by Rick Kuhn and Raghu Kacker of the National Institute of Standards and Technology, Yu Lei of the University of Texas at Arlington, and Justin Hunter of Hexawise[5] (a leading provider of test design software supporting this method), in IEEE Computer magazine[6] describes this method and the benefits realized from its use. Clearly this is an important development that should be widely applied. It is probable this method will rapidly gain "market share" relative to traditional manual test design methods. I have not included modeling of this method here, but models illustrating its impact are provided on the companion web site.

Roles and Responsibilities

Software teams, above all else, must be fully responsible and accountable for software quality. That may seem self-evident but it is certainly not the operational reality today among the 85%. In actual practice the top priority of software teams is schedule. "Are we there yet?" Business leaders, software managers, and the teams themselves are obsessed with getting the software delivered at the earliest possible date. In the rush to finish, quality is a very secondary consideration. In practice, software is delivered when delay is no longer acceptable, irrespective of quality – no one really knows how good or bad it is – "we'll fix it in the next release".

As we have seen, this reality leads to defect containment rates of 85% or less among immature organizations. If you want to improve value-added, reduce cycle time, and lower costs you MUST change the rules. Manage software teams on delivered quality. Set specific containment goals. Provide recognition and rewards for exceptional quality. Cycle time is important, but can improve only if quality comes first! To improve quality formal software inspections are a necessity. Software teams "own" formal inspections – they are not done by others. Formal inspections are NOT audits.

Formal inspections are conducted by peers – i.e., persons regarded by all participants as having knowledge and experience generally equivalent to other participants. All participants must be fluent in the notation and technology being inspected. That means, with few exceptions, managers do not participate. Greenhorns also do not participate, but may observe. Data collected are confidential to the team and are never used to evaluate individuals. Aggregate data is used to manage the process

Formal inspections are win-win activities. Not only do they find defects in the work product being inspected, they also provide near real-time feedback to the inspectors. Learning will inevitably occur that leads to a virtuous loop that results in fewer defects inserted in subsequent development efforts.

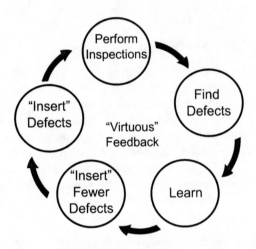

One of the roles in the formal inspection process is a facilitator or leader. Some organizations centralize this role, perhaps within a quality assurance group, and allocate facilitators to teams as required. Personally I do not favor this approach. I believe the facilitator/leader should come from the team developing the product to be inspected – the centralized approach tends to lead to resistance from the teams – they often view the central resource as a spy – "I'm from corporate – I'm here to help". In any event, formal training of all participants is essential. Reading about this process is not enough to ensure effectiveness.

I strongly recommend you establish a "defect czar" (reporting to the "CMO") who is responsible for ensuring availability of necessary infrastructure (defect tracking tools), for ensuring the data are cross-checked and integrated to ensure accuracy, and for preparing summary analyses. This individual will be a good candidate to be the central repository of the defect containment models described below.

Data Collection Requirements

Defect Data

Every defect found by any appraisal method, including those found by customers (internal and/or external) must be recorded in a database if you are serious about improving software outcomes. That does not mean we are going to ask individuals to track every change – unit tests and individual code reviews / walkthroughs are usually not subject to tracking. Once an author declares a work product "complete" however, and releases it for independent appraisal by others, all defects found should be tracked. You are probably spending 60-70% of your software dollars on finding and fixing defects. If you'd rather put some of that money to better use you must come to have a rich understanding of defects.

For every defect you will want to record, at a minimum, how it was found (by a customer or by a specific appraisal step), when it was found (at what stage of the project), where it was found (what place in the item being appraised) and when it was "inserted" ("origin"). Additional information, such as severity and defect type, may also prove valuable. However, make sure the minimum basics are complete and correct before getting too complicated.

Most organizations will have a support group that takes calls and resolves issues related to installed software. Often that is a different group than the software development group – it is often called a "help desk". Most of these organizations have systems to log and track customer requests and trouble reports – some of these reports are software defects, some are not. Some are duplicates; some cannot be reproduced and are attributed to gremlins or the phase of the moon. In some cases the support organization will fix the defect and in other instances they will refer confirmed defects to the development organization for correction.

Most help desk groups will use a software system to keep track of reported and open issues and will gather various statistics. This system will be your primary source for customer reported defects. In most instances the system used to track defects within the development organization is not the same system the help desk uses. We'll not go into that swamp here, but suffice it to say these groups have different needs and it may well make sense for them to use different systems. However, it is also absolutely essential that they can be readily reconciled to ensure an accurate and unduplicated count of defects that are in fact attributable to errors in the software itself.

Many organizations have systems within the development organization that they use to track defects found by testing. Unfortunately many of these systems are extremely leaky – they don't really capture more than a fraction of the actual defects detected. When efforts are made (rarely) to reconcile records of defect-related changes made to the software vs. defect records in the defect tracking system there is often a big difference. Reasons for this reside in the technical swamp and are beyond our scope here. Suffice it to say that this problem is entirely manageable, but it does require a certain level of maturity and discipline. You must have accurate data in order to calculate containment rates. You will never get beyond level 1 or 2 if you don't measure containment!

In several assessment projects I have undertaken we calculated containment rates using available records of customer defects and defects found by testing. We found containment rates in the 50-60% range! If this were actually correct these systems would have been entirely unusable – mean time to failure for systems with those sorts of containment rates would be measured in hours – no one could possibly live with that level of reliability. Hence, the data were certainly wrong. When we drilled down into the software change records we found containment rates were more similar to the expected 85% - not great, but better than it first seemed. When you first start to measure containment you can expect a similar result.

Test Effort Data

To effectively manage our appraisal processes we need to know how much time we spend, in aggregate, on each different type of appraisal activity. As it relates to testing we typically see different types of testing such as "integration", "systems", "acceptance", etc. Ideally we will want to know how much time, in total, is spent on each of these different test types. Even better it would be nice to know how much time was spent planning vs. executing tests - but that can come later and is not essential initially.

In the upcoming section on Cost of Quality we will explore time accounting in general. Given a suitable "chart of accounts" that system will supply what we need as regards aggregate test effort per test type.

Rework Effort Data

Similarly we will want to keep track of aggregate rework effort associated with each appraisal type. Again, that data can come from the Cost of Quality system.

Formal Inspection Data

Formal inspections, as we have seen, are a "defined process" that has, among other things, specific data collection requirements. Data collected are used in a very specific way to monitor and manage the inspection process itself in a virtuous feedback loop that ensures sustained maximum benefit. Data collected by inspections are also used more broadly to control and manage the overall quality process, the key to improving the value-added ratio.

Data collected for each individual inspection event include:

- Number of participants in the inspection (no less than 3, no more than 5)

- Size of the work product inspected (generally limited to around 300-400 lines)

- Time spent in the individual preparation step

    ◊ Used with size to calculate a "prep rate" that is managed to targets known to maximize effectiveness and efficiency

- Time spent in the inspection meeting

    ◊ Used with size to calculate a "meet rate" that is managed to targets known to maximize effectiveness and efficiency

- Number of major and minor defects found

- A list or log of specific defects found and their location

- Origin of the defect if known – e.g., we are inspecting code and determine that a defect originated in an incorrect requirement. This enables, in retrospect, a reasonable estimate of total defects actually present in an earlier phase. When sufficient data have been collected these experienced based data on defect potential replace industry benchmarks.

- Rework hours

- Follow up & close hours

These data are often kept in a database dedicated to inspections data, but in some instances are in the same system used to track test defects. Note however that these data are more detailed and may not be compatible with test records.

Formal inspection data partially overlaps the aggregate information kept in the Cost of Quality system. For example, the sum of total time spent across individual records of requirements inspections should approximately equal requirements appraisal hours recorded in the Cost of Quality system. For reasons too involved to get into here it is generally best to keep inspection data in a separate system from that used for Cost of Quality. To do otherwise unnecessarily complicates and compromises both systems. It's really simpler and more effective to keep two different sets of data, and also important to use them as cross-checks on the accuracy of each.

Effectiveness and Efficiency Metrics

Defect containment effectiveness is measured by a set of defect containment rates.

The "final" containment rate is called "Total Containment Effectiveness" (TCE) – it measures the percentage of total defects removed before the software in released to the customer.

- TCE = DP / (DP + DR)

  where DP = # major defects found pre-release

  DR = # major defects found after release (during an agreed time period)

A series of interim containment rates, called "Appraisal Containment Effectiveness" (ACE_1 ... ACE_n) can be used to measure the effectiveness of each specific type of appraisal. Appraisals will include activities such as requirements, design, and code inspections, static analysis of code, and a series of different types of tests. Effectiveness of a given series of appraisals in aggregate determines TCE.

- ACE_n = DF / DI

  where DF = # major defects found by this appraisal step

  DI = # major defects incoming to this appraisal step

I provide a Defect Containment Model that uses estimates of these rates to both forecast and then monitor defect containment – this model is briefly described in the next section. The model can be used to develop "what if" analyses of various alternatives.

Defect containment efficiency is measured by a set of costs. For each appraisal step we calculate effort to do the appraisal (essentially a "fixed" cost) and rework effort to fix each major defect found (essentially a "variable" cost). Effort (cost) to find defects plus effort (cost) to fix defects = total non-value added effort (cost). Our goal is simple – minimize total non-value added in aggregate across all appraisals.

Defect Containment Econometric Models

These models, sources of parameter values, and associated detailed instructions on their use may be accessed from the companion web site for this book, www.process-fusion.net/blackhole. These models get a bit complicated as they embody moderately complex feed-forward and feed-back loops – you will need to visit the web site to understand the complete story. As this book is intended primarily for executives and managers I have included only the "abridged" version here – just enough to explain what these models are intended to accomplish.

The full model is a bit more involved than illustrated here. It provides for forecasts and also can be used to capture actual results as projects progress. As organizations gain experience they will begin to develop forecasts using locally derived data rather than industry benchmarks.

As with any model, its utility is a function of the assumptions (parameters) used to build the models. I have provide a reasonable "starter set" of default parameters appropriate to a project at the low end of the high risk band. Those interested in using these models will find additional guidelines on selecting parameters and using the models on the web site.

The models I provide consist of five separate tables, each building on its predecessor – the first table, the Defect Containment Model, may be used to forecast the software quality consequences of alternative appraisal mix strategies before the fact, and to document actual results after the fact.

Shaded cells are calculated by the model, other cells are parameters supplied by the model builder. Parameters required for this table include Potential Major Defects (usually a benchmark value initially), and an estimated containment rate per appraisal type (9 of them are included in the default model, but may be changed). If any particular appraisal method will not be used the containment % for that appraisal type is set to zero – i.e., no defects will be removed. Using these values and a "size" parameter (size = 1000 in this example) the model calculates an estimate of defects likely to be found, and an estimate of defects remaining (which includes an allowance for "bad fixes").

Table 1: Defect Containment Model

Appraisal Step		Forecast			
Tag	Description	DI - Potential Major Defects/size "Inserted"	ACE %	DF - Major Defects Found	DR - Major Defects Remaining
ACE1	e.g., Requirements Inspection	.84	60%	504	371
ACE2	e.g., Design Inspection	1.69	60%	1237	911
ACE3	e.g., Code Inspection	1.97	60%	1729	1273
ACE4	e.g., Static Analysis		50%	637	681
ACE5	e.g., Unit Test		0%	0	681
ACE6	e.g., Function Test		0%	0	681
ACE7	e.g., Integration Test		30%	204	491
ACE8	e.g., System Test		35%	172	331
ACE9	e.g., Acceptance Test		25%	83	254
			Total Containment Effectiveness		94.7%

The second table, the Inspection Effort Model, is used to predict required inspection (appraisal) and related rework effort based on parameters that state the modeler's assumptions as to the percentage of the work product to be inspected, the number of defects expected to be found by each different inspection type, and the expected rework hours per defect found. Again we usually begin with benchmark values and revise as we gain experience.

Table 2: Inspection Effort Model

Appraisal Step		Forecast						
Tag	Description	% Inspected	Majors per Inspection	# Inspections	Inspect person months	Rework hours per major defect	Rework person months	Total person months
ACE1	e.g., Requirements Inspection	75%	18.4	15	2.1	0.500	1.9	4.0
ACE2	e.g., Design Inspection	50%	18.4	25	3.4	0.750	7.0	10.4
ACE3	e.g., Code Inspection	20%	3.75	68	9.3	1.000	13.1	22.4
			Totals	108	14.7		22.0	36.7

You will notice this table does not suggest 100% inspection. Experience has shown that defects are not evenly distributed – rather they are "clustered" in certain high risk areas of the various work products. Consequently we can inspect a carefully chosen percentage of the work product and yet find all of the defects projected by the Defect Containment Model described above as Table 1.

Table 3, the Static Analysis Effort Model, requires we provide an estimate of the effort required (per size) to perform the analysis. Using that value, and a size parameter (1000 in this example), total estimated analysis effort is calculated. An additional parameter indicates estimated rework hours per major defect found, and that value is used to calculate estimated rework and total effort associated with defects found by this appraisal method.

Table 3: Static Analysis Effort Model

Appraisal Step		Forecast						
Tag	Description	Hours per size			Analysis person months	Rework hours per major defect	Rework person months	Total person months
ACE4	e.g., Static Analysis (applies to code only)	0.1			0.8	0.250	1.2	2.0
			Totals		0.8		1.2	2.0

Table 4, the Test Effort Model, requires parameters that forecast test hours per size for each test method planned to be used. It also requires a "Pre-Test Impact Factor". This parameter is used to estimate the impact that will result if pre-test appraisals are in fact used. When pre-test methods are used there are several important consequences that impact test effort:

- When pre-test methods are used the number of defects coming into any given test step will necessarily be significantly fewer.

- Hence, fewer defects will be found, and less rework will be needed to correct those defects. "Variable" cost will go down.

- Fewer defects incoming means fewer tests will fail. When a test fails it will often prevent other tests from being executed – they are said to be "blocked".

- Fewer defects incoming also means fewer tests will need to be re-executed to confirm the fix resolved the problem and did not cause unintended secondary effects.

- In total the length of the overall test cycle may be significantly shorter, resulting in a reduction in total labor cost required - "fixed" cost may also be less.

The Pre-Test Impact Factor is used to quantify the overall impact of these consequences – in effect this value indicates the % reduction expected for a given test step due to pre-test appraisals. The value may in some instances be 100% (1.0) if incoming quality is sufficiently good to enable us to simply not do certain types of tests (e.g., unit tests). As we will see this is indeed indicated in some scenarios.

The final parameter required for table 4 is an estimate of rework hours per major defect found by this appraisal. Some authorities suggest this value does not increase significantly as we move through the process, others argue it does. In my experience it does increase, but only slowly.

Table 4: Test Effort Model

Appraisal Step					Forecast			
Tag	Description	Hours per size	Pre-test Impact Factor		Test Execution Person months	Rework hours per major defect	Rework person months	Total person months
ACE5	e.g., Unit Test	0.880	1.000		0.0	1.000	0.0	0.0
ACE6	e.g., Function Test	0.880	1.000		0.0	1.000	0.0	0.0
ACE7	e.g., Integration Test	0.750	0.500		2.8	1.250	1.9	4.8
ACE8	e.g., System Test	0.660	0.500		2.5	1.500	2.0	4.5
ACE9	e.g., Acceptance Test	0.380	0.500		1.4	1.750	1.1	2.5
			Pre-Release Total		6.8		5.0	11.8
			Post-Release Rework			8.0	15.4	15.4
			Project Totals		6.8		20.4	27.2

The final table in the set is a summary of the preceding tables – it provides a forecast of total non-value-added activity for the scenario being modeled.

Table 5: NVA Effort Summary

Appraisal Step					Forecast			
Tag	Description				Appraisal Person months		Rework person months	Total person months
	Total Inspection Effort				14.7		22.0	36.7
	Total Static Analysis				.8		1.2	2.0
	Total Pre-Release Test				6.8		5.0	11.8
			Total Pre-Release NVA		22.2		28.2	50.5
			Post-Release Rework		0.0		15.4	15.4
			Project Totals		22.2		43.6	65.9

By now you may be wondering "ok, so where is all of this going?" Let's take a look at what we can learn from using these models to play out a series of scenarios that embody different appraisal strategies.

Scenario 1 – common practice today – "Test Only" – five types of tests are used

Scenario 2 – "better" – 50% of Code is inspected and the 5 test types are continued

Scenario 3 – "best" – Requirements, Design, and 20% code inspections are used, Static Analysis is added, and the first 2 test types are discontinued

I have defined a "reasonable" set of parameters common to all three scenario models – common containment rates, unit costs for rework, etc. What varies across the different scenarios is the mix of appraisal types included – nothing else changes. Here are the results:

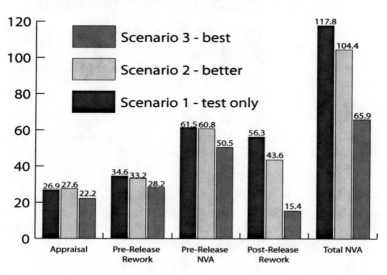

Defect Containment Scenarios

Delivered Quality (TCE)

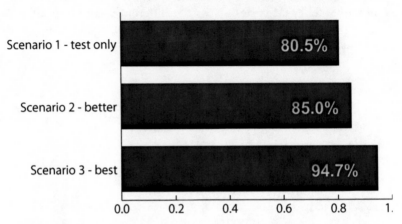

The "best" scenario reduces total NVA by more than 50% compared to "test only" and delivered quality (TCE) improves from 80.5% to over 94.7%!

Even more important, post-release rework is reduced by over 80%! This saves costs in the software team, but also greatly improves the customer experience – fewer interruptions for software defects, more time achieving business goals!

This is NOT speculation – YOU CAN DO THIS – better, faster, AND cheaper.

Implementation Considerations

Appropriate infrastructure to support collection and reporting of defect data will be required. If you outsource development the supplier will typically provide the infrastructure, but if not you must make appropriate arrangements internally.

Predict and Measure Defect Containment "Take-aways"

- To increase value-added, the single most important thing any software organization can do is to apply an appropriate amount of resource, using appropriate Appraisal methods, at every stage of the development process.

- To effectively manage defect containment every organization must predict the number of defects likely to be "inserted" at each stage of the development process. Most will rely initially on industry benchmarks and revise as experience is gained.

- A count of defects discovered can be compared to the estimate of defects present to approximate a "containment rate" at each stage of development. This rate is a leading indicator that provides useful insight into product quality as the project progresses. This metric, in effect, provides a "quality adjusted" view of project status.

- Available Appraisal methods include not only testing, widely used in most organizations, but also a variety of pre-test methods, including formal software inspections and, where applicable, static analysis. Pre-test methods are dramatically more effective and efficient than the "test only" approach commonly used.

- Collection and analysis of defect data provides critical feedback essential to improvement. The details of how to do that and ensure data quality require you assign a "defect czar" (ideally reporting to the "CMO"), to monitor, maintain, analyze, and report.

- Require reporting of defect related efficiency and effectiveness metrics, including Total Containment Effectiveness (TCE) and Appraisal Containment Effectiveness (ACE) for each Appraisal method.

- Require use of the Defect Containment Econometric Models proposed here, or equivalent. These models enable forecasting of the consequences of different defect insertion and detection rates, rework costs, and alternative Appraisal strategies.

In aggregate these models forecast and monitor the impact of defect containment strategies as they drive non-value-added cost.

- As illustrated above, following the recommendations I have made and using the data collected in a virtuous feedback loop will lead to a 40% reduction in non-value-added effort over a period of perhaps two years. Longer term you can expect to realize additional gains. At the same time you reduce non-value-added you will simultaneously reduce delivered defects by 60-80%!

Monitor Cost of Quality

Executive Summary

Software and IT suffer from a curious malady – one the one hand, too much measurement, and on the other, too little. Most General Managers have a very hard time getting a clear idea what the net impacts of the plethora of lower-level measures actually are. It is not my intent to claim the suggestions here are a complete solution to all needs, just a very good place to start separating the forest from the trees.

Where Does the Time Go?

As we discussed in Part 2, much of the information organizations have about labor utilization is unreliable.

1. Reliability of the data is inversely proportional to the number of charge categories. More categories mean more entries for each individual and more time to do the reporting. Most individuals will enter time weekly or even less often, and cannot accurately remember how time was actually spent. Many individuals will do development and support activities in the same week, work on several development projects, and several phases/tasks within each – commonly one person will spend time on dozens of different charge categories. In a majority of software and

IT organizations the total hours reported differ greatly from a simple crosscheck of headcount times potentially available hours – often indicating under reporting of 20% or more.

2. Many de-facto incentives exist that distort the data – to mention just one, it is common practice to stop charging time to a project when the budget has run out – instead, time is charged to something that has remaining budget, independent of the actual work being performed. Similar distortions occur between phases. The infamous "hear no evil, see no evil" conspiracy prevails. Those who want to know the reality are often frustrated by those who would rather obscure it.

3. There is usually no feedback to the individuals reporting time, and no decisions typically result – hence, widespread cynicism becomes entrenched – "nobody uses this data, so who cares". Non-compliance and distortion become the norm.

Less is More

From an efficiency improvement perspective task level time detail is not useful, because that data is not comparable across projects. What is common to all projects, and far more useful for measuring efficiency, is a "Cost of Quality (CoQ)[7]" view of time expenditures. For software and IT activities we commonly use a simplified three part CoQ scheme consisting of Appraisal (testing, inspections, any activity performed to find defects), Rework (all effort expended to correct defects detected by Appraisals and by customers), and Value Added, which is simply total time less Appraisal and Rework – collectively referred to as "internal" CoQ.

Significant additional costs, known as "external" CoQ, include all costs incurred by the development and/or support organizations associated with diagnosis and correction of defects released to customers. External CoQ should also include the costs experienced by the customer as a consequence of defects, but in practice these are very difficult to measure and are often ignored. Some estimates suggest these costs are roughly equal to internal CoQ.

In many instances this approach will mean less time reporting, not more – fewer items in the "Chart of Accounts" (list of time-charge categories). Alternately, if you are committed to more detailed task level time accounting you can structure your chart of accounts so that the detail is explicitly mapped to CoQ categories.

Appraisal is all time spent finding defects – in most organizations this is primarily testing, but may also include inspections and reviews of various work products prior to testing. Most organizations plan to devote 30-40% of total effort to this activity, but usually have no idea if that is enough or too much. Testing usually stops when time runs out with little or no insight into the effectiveness of effort expended.

Appraisals, once you decide to do them, can be regarded as "fixed" costs – i.e., that effort will be expended even if no defects are found.

Rework is all time spent fixing defects found by any form of appraisal and/or by customers after a system is delivered - typically 30-40% of total effort, but rarely measured. Rework is always a variable cost that is a function of the number of defects actually found. To predict that you must make some estimate (implicit or explicit) of the number of defects you expect to find.

Most 85% organizations cannot separate Appraisal effort from Rework effort.

Value Added is simply total time spent minus time spent on Appraisal and Rework. When measured, which rarely occurs, Value Added is commonly 30% of total effort.

Improving efficiency, simply put, means increasing value added! Any and all improvement initiatives can set goals and measure improvements in terms of impact on Value Added – which occurs when Appraisal and Rework are reduced.

Note that this definition of Value Added is offered for the sake of "operational definition" simplicity – it does not exclude the possibility that some effort categorized as Value Added may by redundant or unnecessary. However, let's eat the elephant one bite at a time – when we get Value Added to 50% or less we can begin to consider refinements of our categories.

Implementation Considerations

The internal politics of Cost of Quality implementation often prove complex. I have proposed an approach to dealing with these issues in some detail. One of the keys to success is to appoint someone with sufficient independence and authority to lead the effort. I suggest appointment of a "Chief Measurement Officer" to shepherd implementation and reporting of metrics generally and Cost of Quality specifically. I also discuss how a Cost of Quality framework can be used to drive improvement throughout the organization by apportioning goals to lower levels.

Roles and Responsibilities

1. Design – someone must design a standard "chart of accounts" that will be used across the organization to report effort into the cost of quality time accounting system. An example is provided below under "Implementation Considerations". Responsibility for this activity should be assigned to the same individual or group responsible for "auditing" to ensure accuracy and for reporting. I suggest you give serious consideration to appointing a "Chief Measurement Officer" (CMO) or equivalent reporting to a sufficiently high level in the organization to ensure independence and objectivity. This responsibility should not be assigned to anyone within or directly accountable for performance of the development organization, whether internal or outsourced.

   The "CMO" must take care to facilitate, not dictate, the details of this design. The CMO must ensure those reporting fully understand the design and are given opportunities to review and object if they do not feel the scheme proposed fairly represents their legitimate interests.

2. Audit and reporting – The CMO or equivalent must perform sanity checks and audits to confirm the accuracy and

completeness of reported data. Those reporting, and their managers, should be given private feedback and help to ensure accuracy and completeness. Only as a last resort does the CMO "go public" with issues. Ultimately, best results are realized when a "win-win" relationship is created. Periodic comprehensive reports of actual results should be provided to all stakeholders. In general a positive climate will result when results for individual groups are kept confidential to that group. Unidentified comparisons and rankings are useful, but making anyone look bad publicly does not generally lead to desired outcomes. Help the laggards, praise and reward the leaders.

3. Tools – some IT group, probably one that already exists, will be required to configure and support the tools that are used to collect the data. Most of these groups today are comparatively low level technical types. They know in depth how the tools work and how to configure them. Very few of them know the origin of or reason for the configurations they prepare and support. Many existing systems produce hundreds of reports and queries that have been built up over many years. Frequently no one really knows why all this stuff exists or how it is used. Making changes can have unexpected consequences. Often there is heavy resistance to making significant changes. You will likely need some leverage.

4. Data entry – the teams doing the work are necessarily those who will provide that data. They must bear ultimate responsibility for its accuracy and completeness. Make sure they understand the chart of accounts and how you intend to use the data. Make it clear accuracy and completeness are a job requirement, just like honest accounting for travel expenses. This is fiduciary responsibility 101!

Implementation Considerations

Every organization that attempts improvement based on measurement invariably runs up against resistance. Often that is written off to "politics" and dismissed as an impossible problem to solve – it's just too hard - let's just give up.

Sometimes it's useful to reflect for a moment on the fact that the word "politics" has the same root as the word "polite", and to realize that resistance is frequently a consequence of a lack of careful, tactful, consideration of potential impacts of measurements on those they measure. Imposing any set of metrics, however valid or well intentioned, is almost always a recipe for disaster – understanding and trust must come first.

Let's face it – nobody really wants to be measured. Meaningful measurement just does not happen unless the reasons for measures and their intended uses are made clear and are mandatory. Most software and IT organizations measure lots of 'stuff', but very few are clear about why they measure, and even fewer actually make meaningful use of the measures they collect. Most organizations have too many measures, and make too little use of them. The approach proposed here seeks to get to the core issue for most organizations – i.e., "How can we set up a simple and economical measurement framework that is common across the organization, motivates improvement, and allows us to show our business partners we are getting 'better, faster, and cheaper'?"

Before you start any measurement initiative make very sure you have solid executive sponsorship – you can be sure this process will generate controversy and contention. Arrange for a C-level executive to communicate the intent of this process to all who will be involved – solicit openness and cooperation – make it clear you intend to reduce or eliminate any existing measures that are not valuable. While every organization is somewhat different, there are perhaps some common themes that facilitate successful implementation of a cost of quality framework in most instances.

Step 1: Identify an Executive Sponsor

Success will depend fundamentally on finding an executive sponsor willing to put 'skin in the game' – passive cheer-leading is NOT enough. Sorry, but you'll never get anywhere trying to drive measurement from below or beside those who will collect and use the data. You MUST have executive sponsorship. Worse yet, your executive sponsor must "get it" and be prepared to be patient and supportive over an extended period. Cost of Quality (or any other measurement system) is NOT a silver bullet – it will take time to get real valid results. You need your executive sponsor to communicate her/his sponsorship, intentions, and understanding.

Something like the following sample kick-off communication may work:

To:	All IT Colleagues
From:	"The Chief"
Re:	Cost of Quality

As all of you are aware, our business partners expect continuous improvement in everything we do – we've all heard the "better, faster, cheaper" mantra. We have for some time been searching for a way to measure and demonstrate our improvement that is common across the organization, and believe a relatively simple approach known as "Cost of Quality" will provide the framework. I believe this approach will work in all areas of IT. Successful implementation of this approach will require your cooperation and good will. I want to assure you that this program will be used in a strictly constructive way – not to find fault with anyone, but to help all of us improve our performance and demonstrate that improvement to our business partners.

Over the next several months a team will be conducting a series of facilitated sessions designed to inventory all of the measures we currently have. With your cooperation we will evaluate the value of these measures and develop the details necessary to implemen a simplified and improved measurement program in a fair and practical manner. You will be fully informed about the objectives and processes involved. Your input will be solicited and will have a major influence on how we execute this.

In broad outline our plan and schedule for implementation of this program will be approximately as follows, subject of course to adjustments if needed:

Step 1: Inventory and Evaluate Existing Measures.(~2 months)

Step 2: Establish and/or Update Measurement Policy.(~1 month)

Step 3: Establish Baselines and Set Targets. (~ 6 months)

No immediate actions will be taken on this data, but my expectation is that each group manager will be prepared to indicate at the end of this period that they are confident they have accurate baseline values for the data collected. It is the responsibility of each manager and group to ensure they have an accurate baseline at the end of the baseline period.

Targets will then be developed in a collaborative manner, engaging those impacted. Each group manager, together with his or her team, will be expected to define specific improvement targets for Cost of Quality metrics, with the overall intention that each group will improve their "Value Added" contribution relative to the baselines established during the startup period. These goals will be incorporated in all managers and groups MBO goals for future periods.

Step 4: Formulate Improvement Plans to Achieve Targets; Determine Priorities. (~ 3 months) The quality team will assist each group as appropriate.

Step 5: Evaluate Achievements Using the Agreed Measures. (Quarterly and Annually)

No doubt many will want to make this happen faster. Many have tried, few have succeeded – this is a race the tortoise nearly always wins. Getting this operational in six months would be a triumph – 12 months is probably more likely.

Step 2: Inventory and Evaluate Existing Measures

Make a comprehensive list of all measurements currently collected. Identify any policies related to these measures.

- Determine the reason for each measure. (e.g., Chargeback, Sox)

- Who uses them? To whom are results reported? A comprehensive catalog of sample reports or other measurement outputs should be compiled, indicating who receives each and what they do with them. What actions or decisions are taken based on each measure? Concrete examples should be documented.

- What would be the consequence if any measure were to be discontinued? Do those collecting and using the measures believe they should be continued as they are? Would they propose changes that may reduce cost or improve usability or value?

- Are the measures reasonably formulated? (e.g., are averages used for SLAs when percentiles would be more appropriate?)

- How much effort is required to collect and process each measure? Does the cost/benefit make sense?

- How granular are the measures? Is the level of detail appropriate? (e.g., is task level reporting on projects really useful?) Are the measures as simple as they can be?

- What incentives (formal or informal, positive or negative) are in place that may influence the validity of any measures? Do in-place incentives motivate desired behavior?

- Are measures used fairly and appropriately? Can examples of misuse be identified?

    To make this review useful it will be important to probe below the surface to get past "this is the way we've always done it". If this review is undertaken with an open mind and is not simply a superficial exercise, it is very probable that a number of measures can be discontinued or simplified to reduce related expense.

Results of this review and any recommendations arising from it should be comprehensively reviewed with responsible executives and stakeholders.

Step 3: Establish or Update Measurement Policy

Most C-level executives will be amazed and appalled by the results of the Step 2 review. It will provide a great opportunity to apply the type of thinking that underlies "zero base budgeting" – i.e., just because we have always done something is not in itself a justification for continuing. If not annually at least periodically it is appropriate to 'review the bidding' and question why we are doing many of the things we do.

The end result of such a review should be creation or re-statement of a policy mandate that clearly defines the "what" and "why" for measurement. What should this policy mandate include?

- A statement of measurement program objectives. (Why we measure) e.g., chargeback, status tracking, process improvement (increasing value-add), quality management, SLA management, etc.

- A list of the items that are to be measured. (What we measure) At a minimum, every organization should measure effort (person hours), defects, workload / backlog and schedule performance (planned and actual durations).

- A requirement that all effort be categorized using a "Cost of Quality" framework – i.e., value added, appraisal, rework, and process improvement. This is an essential foundation for process improvement. Few organizations measure this today, and most are astonished when they do so. Typical software development and deployment activities realize less than 40% value-added effort.

- A "protocol" that defines appropriate uses of measures. Remembering Deming's "Drive Out Fear" it is generally appropriate to use measures to improve processes, but not to evaluate individuals. Exceptions to this general rule may be appropriate for managers when MBOs are based on measures and appropriate steps are taken to ensure the accuracy of data.

- A plan and schedule for deployment. Deployment begins with a communication of the policy statement that has been formulated, reflecting the choices and decisions you have made.

- A requirement that a 'chart of accounts' be established and approved for effort tracking. Most organizations use a too-detailed structure that adds overhead and leads to inaccuracies. When creating a chart of accounts for effort tracking, "more is less". More items in the chart of accounts invariably reduce the level of compliance and the accuracy of the data as individuals find they are required to make dozens of different entries every week and simply cannot maintain accuracy.

A sample project chart of accounts is illustrated below. All projects use a set of accounts that are common and standardized across all projects, but any given project may use only a subset as appropriate to the project.

Sample Cost of Quality Time Accounting "Project Chart of Accounts"		
Phase	**Activity**	**Description**
e.g., Requirements	V1- Value Added Effort	All requirements related effort that is NOT Appraisal or Rework
	A1 – e.g., Requirements Inspection	Each unique type of Appraisal is assigned a unique identifier (e.g., "A1") common across all projects – any given project may or may not include a particular Appraisal type.
	R1 – e.g., Requirements Rework	Each Rework account is uniquely associated with a specific Appraisal type
e.g., Design	V2-Value Added Effort	Design effort x- Appraisal & Rework
	A2 – e.g., Design Inspection	Each unique type of Appraisal is assigned a unique identifier common across all projects – any given project may or may not include a particular Appraisal type.
	R2 – e.g., Design Rework	Each Rework account is uniquely associated with a specific Appraisal type
e.g., Construction	V3- Value Added Effort	Construction effort x- Appraisal & Rework
	A3 – e.g., Construction Appraisal	Each unique type of Appraisal is assigned a unique identifier common across all projects – any given project may or may not include a particular Appraisal type.
	R3 – e.g., Construction Rework	Each Rework account is uniquely associated with a specific Appraisal type

e.g., Testing	A4 e.g., Unit Testing	Each unique type of Appraisal is assigned a unique identifier common across all projects – any given project may or may not include a particular Appraisal type.
	R4 e.g., Unit Test Rework	Each Rework account is uniquely associated with a specific Appraisal type
	A5 e.g., Function Test	Each unique type of Appraisal is assigned a unique identifier common across all projects – any given project may or may not include a particular Appraisal type.
	R5 e.g., Function Test Rework	Each Rework account is uniquely associated with a specific Appraisal type
	A6 e.g., Integration Test	Each unique type of Appraisal is assigned a unique identifier common across all projects – any given project may or may not include a particular Appraisal type.
	R6 e.g., Integration Test Rework	Each Rework account is uniquely associated with a specific Appraisal type
	A7 e.g., System Test	Each unique type of Appraisal is assigned a unique identifier common across all projects – any given project may or may not include a particular Appraisal type.
	R7 e.g., System Test Rework	Each Rework account is uniquely associated with a specific Appraisal type
	A8 e.g., Acceptance Test	Each unique type of Appraisal is assigned a unique identifier common across all projects – any given project may or may not include a particular Appraisal type.
	R8 e.g., Acceptance Test Rework	Each Rework account is uniquely associated with a specific Appraisal type

In most organizations effort accounting and schedule management are combined in a single system that is neither "fish nor fowl". Far better in most instances to separate the tracking of effort and schedule – only organizations with very mature project management processes and a need to use Earned Value should attempt effort tracking at a task level.

Step 4: Establish Baselines and Set Targets

- Spend time educating all concerned on the basic Cost of Quality definitions. Allow each group to develop specific examples in their current work. Be prepared to answer some difficult questions and to develop precise yet simple "operational definitions" that are widely accepted. Make sure everyone has a clear understanding of what the data mean before anything is actually collected. If it's not simple it won't be effective.

- Work with those involved to define how data will be collected, recognizing that the overhead involved must be reasonable to have any chance of success. It is ESSENTIAL that you build in data validation from the start. If you don't have a continuous validation process you can be sure the data will not be accurate. Make the local managers responsible for accuracy – after all, they are going to be expected to demonstrate improvement in the future, so the old "the data isn't accurate" excuse must be off the table.

- Pilot the data collection and validation processes and tools – be prepared to make changes to iron out difficulties. DON'T be married to "but that's just the way our tracking system is designed." Any package you may be using has lots of flexibility – you CAN reconfigure if you want to – "do what you always did, get what you always got". Keep it simple.

- Collect the baseline data. It is very unlikely that data you collect today is accurate enough to be useful as a baseline – some will argue with that, but at a minimum it is essential to sanity check to see what the facts are. A simple test like cross-checking total hours reported each week against headcount times 40 usually reveals a serious gap. The gap gets bigger when you start to check how time is allocated to projects – the lower you go into the detail, the worse it gets. Publish frequent feedback on the facts you have found. Expect questions and challenges.

Step 5: Formulate Improvement Plans to Achieve Targets; Determine Priorities

- Prepare an educational program to provide illustrations of how to interpret the data and to provide some ideas that might be used to drive improvement. Best results invariably come from initiatives that originate among those "being improved" – it helps to educate them on possibilities, but best for them to make their own choices within the frame of overall objectives set by executive management – tell them what you expect them to achieve, not how to get it done. Reward positive results – learning will quickly follow.

Step 6: Evaluate Achievements

- Collect the data, ensuring on-going evaluation of data quality and continuous feedback to those collecting and using the data.

- Apply Lean Six Sigma methods to evaluate changes for statistical significance. More on that in the section entitled Focusing on Performance, not Compliance

- If targets are not being achieved, provide assistance to determine root causes and refine improvement strategies.

- Provide rewards and/or recognition to those who achieve targets.

Monitor Cost of Quality "Take-aways"

Many organizations collect task level time accounting information that is highly inaccurate and rarely used. A simplified data collection chart of accounts will prove more useful and more accurate.

A "Cost of Quality" chart of accounts will collect time in broader categories of Value-Added, Appraisal, Rework, and perhaps Prevention. Monitoring the value-added percentage gives a solid indication of overall improvement.

The Chief Measurement Officer should facilitate definition of an appropriate chart of accounts and report objectively on the data, but responsibility for data accuracy and completeness must rest with those reporting.

The politics of implementation are complex and likely to meet resistance. Clear executive level sponsorship is essential, as is a carefully considered implementation plan. Suggestions are provided in the foregoing.

Focus on Performance, not Compliance

Software professionals, especially those working in regulated environments and in the government sector, face a somewhat bewildering array of relevant standards and best practices. Many of these standards, including ISO and the Software Engineering Institute's Capability Maturity Model, often in practice (if not in principle) place more emphasis on compliance with the standard rather than on actual performance. Many within the SEI have expressed concern about over-emphasis on the rating alone. Certainly level rating is important for government contracting organizations, but is not sufficient by itself to quantitatively demonstrate improved outcomes in terms of cost, quality, or cycle time. Lean Six Sigma, on the other hand, places primary emphasis on understanding and managing performance (outcomes).

As awareness and penetration of Lean Six Sigma in the software world has increased significantly over the last several years, I find many organizations struggling to understand and leverage the relationships between ISO, Lean Six Sigma and several other approaches to software process improvement, including CMMI®. In my view the cases described in a CrossTalk article[8] I co-authored, and other industry experience, answer in the affirmative three questions we hear quite frequently:

• We are already doing Six Sigma; does it make sense to do CMMI® as well? *Clearly each of the cases described felt there was additional value to be gained from engaging CMMI® in addition to Six Sigma – in some instances because CMMI was required by a customer.*

- We are probably CMMI® (staged) level 2 or 3; does it make sense to do Six Sigma before we get to level 4? *None of these organizations described in the cases cited had reached level 4, but all had realized benefits from Six Sigma at lower levels.*

- Management wants us to get to level 5 as soon as possible; can Six Sigma help us get there quicker, or will it slow us down? *Case 3, as well as other results reported in the literature, clearly demonstrates Six Sigma can reduce the time needed to move to higher maturity levels.*

Answering a fourth common question necessarily moves into the realm of opinion – the following is mine:

- We are just getting started on process improvement; should we do Six Sigma, CMMI®, or both? At the same time, or one or the other first? – *My experience convinces me that most organizations will get measurable business results more quickly with Six Sigma than with CMMI®, but ultimately will need the additional insights available from CMMI® to realize maximum benefit. Government contracting organizations will in most cases need to do both in parallel - CMMI® to satisfy government bid requirements and Six Sigma to ensure tight and near-term linkage to measurable business results. Even when CMMI® comes first, level 4 and 5 will invariably lead organizations to something that is very like Six Sigma, even if by another name.*

Many software groups, especially those required to comply with standards in regulated industries, have "software quality assurance" groups who independently review software work products for compliance with applicable standards. In practice these activities are almost entirely focused on compliance and have little to do with delivered product quality. Clearly, while often necessary and unavoidable, these activities are not value-added. Typically they have little impact on efficiency or effectiveness of the software development organization.

A Management Control "Dashboard" for High Risk Projects

If I were responsible for executive oversight of a high risk project I would expect and require the "CMO", with all necessary cooperation from the software team, to provide the following at least monthly:

- Original and Current estimate of project size.

- A list of requested, pending, and approved changes in scope /size. If in aggregate the rate of growth is in excess of 1% per month I would probe deeply into the reasons. Excessive growth is asking for trouble.

- Earned Value "lite" as described earlier. If schedule and/or cost variance exceeds 5% I would expect to see proposed actions to avoid additional variance.

- Planned vs. actual appraisal effort to date and planned vs. actual major defects found to date. Stephen Kan[9] has suggested combining these data in a matrix format as adapted here:

Appraisal Assessment		Defect Rate	
		Higher than Plan	Lower than Plan
Appraisal Effort	Higher than Plan	Defect Potential higher than plan, but many found -"OK"	Best Case - High incoming quality, enough effort to be sure.
	Lower than Plan	Worst Case - Many defects present, insufficient effort devoted to removal	Unclear-incoming quality may have been good; no inspections?

- Planned vs. actual Rework per defect to date
- Original and current estimate of total effort by phase

This information provides a solid understanding of the true status and health of the project. All of these data should be archived and subjected to a thorough "after action" analysis. Lessons learned, and especially the values of key measures, should be widely circulated and used in an on-going education program to reduce future defect insertion and improve defect detection effectiveness and efficiency.

Management by Fact

The current state of the art in proven process improvement methods is defined by the synthesis of Lean and Six Sigma, collectively known as "Lean Six Sigma", hereinafter, "LSS".

"Y" – an outcome, a dependent variable (not directly controllable)

"f" – a function or relationship

x_n – a controllable factor, an independent variable

$$Y = f(x_1 + x_2 + x_3 \ldots)$$

This deceptively simple formula describes the essence of Lean Six Sigma thinking. Simply stated it means that we can identify any desired outcome (a "Y") and employ Lean Six Sigma (or other) methods to identify and quantify the relative impact of the root cause factors (x's) that determine a particular outcome. Throughout Part 3 we have discussed how to make improvements in software project and organizational outcomes by identifying the most important Ys and x's and describing the "functions" that connect them.

Ys and x's can be understood as a hierarchy that can be connected top to bottom. There are a great many potential Ys and x's, but here we will focus on a few of the most important in relation to software projects and organizations. Organizations that understand and apply this sort of quantitative thinking will prosper, those that do not will suffer.

Viewed from the top the most important Y for software (sometimes called the "big Y") is "Value Added %" – i.e., the percentage of our most expensive resource, staff labor, that is not "Non-Value-Added". Non-Valued-Added is in turn a function of total defect containment effectiveness (TCE – we might call that a "small y"), which is in turn a function of appraisal containment effectiveness (ACE). Appraisal methods themselves are also subject to similar thinking. We've examined containment issues and metrics in the section on defect containment.

$$Y \text{ (Valued-Added \%)} = f [x_1 \text{ 100\% (Total Software Labor Cost)} - x_2 \text{ (Non-Value \%)}]$$

$$y \text{ (Total Containment Effectiveness, TCE)} = f [ACE_1 + ACE_2 \ldots]$$

$$y \text{ (ACE)} = f [\text{Appraisal method} + \text{Appraisal effort} + \text{Appraisal effectiveness}]$$

As illustrated above it is always possible to decompose high level outcomes ("Ys") to lower level outcomes ("little ys") and ultimately to root cause factors, the x's. LSS DMAIC (Define-Measure-Analyze-Improve-Control) is clearly the state of the art method for finding root causes, improving processes, and institutionalizing solutions so they are sustained.

LSS is virtually universally applied to manufacturing and also widely used in services to measure and dramatically improve a wide range of products and services. Application of this proven method to software and IT is much less common outside of the best in class 15%.

In part this is due to the fact that many of the "traditional" assumptions underlying LSS often do not fully apply to software organizations. In particular, software processes are not nearly as standardized and fully repeatable as are most manufacturing processes and many transactional processes as well. In addition, software processes are not measureable with the precision usually feasible for manufacturing processes. Software processes are far less subject to precise control – humans do software work and are not finely adjustable with micrometers or volt meters.

Despite these important differences, a "low calorie" approach to Lean Six Sigma that embodies a "Lean" training strategy has proven very effective in software groups. A "low calorie" approach focuses on the core 20% of the body of knowledge, delivered "just in time" with immediate application. Experience shows that the core ideas will deliver 80% of the potential benefit – a classic application of the Pareto principle.

In software groups a "Green Belt" level of training (typically 4-5 days) has proven highly effective. Full time dedicated "Black Belts" are generally not needed.

Six Sigma Understands Variation

Software industry benchmark data, and also data locally collected, can provide a useful frame of reference for baseline assessments and targets, but must be used with great care. Here we illustrate a typical example of the variation inherent in such data.

"Productivity" (units/month)	% in range	"Cause"
75-100	1%	"Special Cause"
50-75	2%	
25-50	3%	
15-25	20%	"Common Cause"
5-15	55%	
1-5	15%	
< 1	4%	"Special Cause"

Source: Applied Software Measurement, 3rd Ed. p.269

We have somewhat arbitrarily labeled the extremes of this data as due to "Special Cause" variation - i.e., we assume there is some exceptional, out of the ordinary explanation for these instances - e.g., measurement errors, projects put on hold, major changes in requirements or other factors not identified.

We assume the central 90% is representative of "Common Cause" or normal process variation - we expect 90% of projects will fall in this range (which is still quite large). According to this data, a 1000 Function Point project will require between 40 and 1000 person months of effort!

If, as a "thought experiment", we generate a random set of project productivity results covering the 'common cause' portion of Jones' data, using his distributions as a guide, we may see a distribution such as that illustrated below. (Remember, this is NOT real data.)

This 'simulation' suggests a mean or average value of 11.1 function points per person month with a standard deviation of 6.1 - in other words, we expect productivity to be in the range of about 5 to 17 FP/PM 67% of the time. Total effort for a 1000 FP project may be expected to range from around 60 to 200 person months - not very comforting! Real data will often exhibit similar characteristics. Automated estimating tools overcome these challenges by incorporating many adjustment factors that narrow the range of variation.

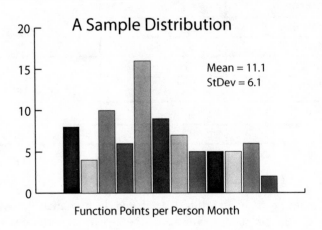

Similar variation will occur in most software related data, including potential defects, defect containment rates, rework effort per defect, etc. All of these variables are subject to significant variation. While not critically necessary at the outset, it becomes increasingly important over time to become "quantitatively literate" if you are serious about management by fact. Over-simplistic use of averages without understanding of variation can lead to many false conclusions. Virtually all of the mature 15% are quantitatively literate and leverage that understanding to achieve continuous improvement.

Many elements from the Six Sigma toolkit have been effectively applied to a wide range of software and IT processes. Most often deployed within the DMAIC framework, tools most widely used include:

- Failure Modes and Effects Analysis (FMEA)

- Pareto Analysis

- Measurement Systems Analysis/Design (MSA/D)

- Hypothesis testing

- Design of Experiments

- Cause and Effect analysis (Ishikawa diagrams)

- Segmentation & Stratification

- Model Building, Regression Analysis

- Nominal Group Technique (NGT)

- Pugh Concept Selection

- Statistical Process Control

Lean Understands Waste

Lean, as it applies to software and IT, is concerned primarily with reduction of the "7 wastes" and with reduction in cycle time (typically a result of removing waste). As mentioned earlier, I suggest you begin with a simple definition of "value-added" – i.e., total effort less Appraisal and Rework. Longer term, however, it will become more important to take a closer look at the value-added portion, as my initial definition does not exclude the possibility that some of the effort initially described as value-added does in fact contain a certain portion of waste.

Shigeo Shingo's Seven Wastes[10]	
Manufacturing	Software Development
In-process Inventory	Incomplete Work
Over-production	Un-needed "features"
Extra Processing	Relearning
Transportation	Handoffs
Motion	Task Switching
Waiting	Waiting
Defects	Defects

As applied to software and IT the most commonly used technique to identify and attack the 7 wastes is Value Stream Analysis in which we develop process maps and measure and analyze each process step from a waste perspective.

Focus on Performance "Take-aways"

A focus on performance is a longer term culture change for most organizations. Quantitative literacy takes time and experience to mature into a way of life.

Implementing the recommendations offered in this book will establish a solid foundation for additional substantial improvement. Applying state of the art methods such as Lean and Six Sigma will lead to continuous improvement. "In Conclusion" I illustrate what you can expect longer term.

In Conclusion ...

A Pound of Prevention

Estimating and planning deficiencies set us up to fail. We must take the necessary time to prepare effectively for every high risk project. The dreaded three-minute mile must be avoided. Deadlines must never be imposed – if you cannot live with the estimate that results from a professional planning and estimating process *don't do the project.*

In addition, effective execution means establishing mechanisms to provide a realistic understanding of project status on a weekly basis. At a minimum we should expect Earned Value lite on a weekly basis in addition to regular reports on planned vs. actual appraisal effort, rework effort, planned vs. actual defects found, and current estimates of defect containment rates for each appraisal type. When significant variances are noted corrective actions are generally indicated. Professionalizing estimating and planning means we must ...

- Determine a "first approximation" size to determine whether or not a proposed project is likely to be in the high risk zone.

- High risk projects must take the time necessary to determine sufficient detail about what is required to enable an expert to determine size to a reasonable level of confidence.

- Given the requirements it is essential to insist upon two independent estimates – one "top down" prepared by a qualified expert not responsible for the development – and another "bottom up" prepared by the development team. Both estimates must leverage appropriate tools. Bottom up estimates must use Critical Path Method and adhere to other guidelines discussed in Part 3. Most critically, small tasks and explicit allowance for appraisal and rework.

- The two estimates must be reconciled. Differences in assumptions must be explored and adjusted until the independent estimates converge.

- Never give approval to start design and development until estimates converge.

Five Pounds of Cure

No matter how effective the planning, execution effectiveness is equally essential. Executing doesn't have a chance if the estimates and plans are poor, but solid plans and estimates do not themselves guarantee happy outcomes.

Effective execution means allocating sufficient effort and employing appropriate appraisal methods at every stage of a project – "early and often". It also means rigorous data collection to enable proactive management of appraisal effectiveness.

In addition, effective execution means establishing mechanisms to provide a realistic understanding of project status on a weekly basis. At a minimum we should expect Earned Value lite on a weekly basis in addition to regular reports on planned vs. actual appraisal effort, rework effort, planned vs. actual defects found, and current estimates of defect containment rates for each appraisal type. When significant variances are noted corrective actions are generally indicated.

Ten Pounds of Learning

Defect tracking and Cost of Quality reporting provide the essential "virtuous feedback" we need to learn and improve. All of the redeeming virtues are intimately inter-connected.

- Early appraisals enable early learning – early containment rates are leading indicators that forecast what is likely to occur later. We can adjust and adapt soon enough to influence outcomes. Finding out we are in trouble when testing starts is too late to take corrective action.

- Defect tracking enables effective process management of the appraisal processes themselves. We know, for example, that containment effectiveness and efficiency of formal inspections are determined by a small set of "critical x's" – i.e., size of material inspected, number of inspectors, preparation rate, and meeting rate. All of these are easily controllable IF we collect the necessary data and use it to monitor and control appraisals in near real time.

- Defect tracking, combined with the data we get from the cost of quality system, enables "large loop" learning. As we begin to have solid facts and data about what actually occurs and what it costs we begin to improve future estimates and lower potential defects. A continuous learning loop is operationalized.

The defect containment models introduced earlier can also be used to show the longer term impact of the learning that occurs as a result of our increased understanding of defect insertion, defect removal, and cost of quality. Several specific consequences result:

- We use what we have learned about defects to educate development teams about what goes wrong at each stage of the development process and to help them learn how to avoid inserting defects. Experience shows this works – the best in class groups insert around 1/3 fewer defects than do the 85% group.

- In addition to inserting fewer defects, groups become better at finding the defects that do occur – effectiveness improves.

- Over a longer term efficiency also improves – inspections use less labor and testing requires fewer test cases.

The chart below illustrates the impact this learning will have in practice. This chart, derived from the same models discussed earlier, assumes we sustain the "scenario 3" appraisal practices, appraisal efficiency and effectiveness are unchanged, but we insert fewer defects. The model parameters we used earlier assumed defects were inserted at a rate of 4.5 per "function point" – a US average benchmark for the 85%.

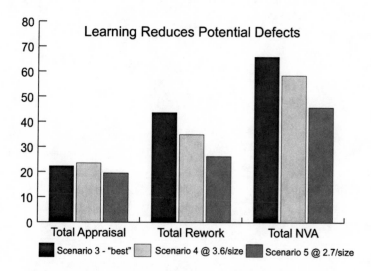

This chart illustrates the impact of successive reductions in insertion to 3.6 per function point (scenario 4) and then to 2.7 per function point (scenario 5). As we see this leads to a further significant reduction in non-value-added effort. As we get better at finding defects, and use less effort to do so, the picture will improve even further. These results are consistent with actual experience among the high maturity 15%.

Fifty Pounds of Benefits

Consistent application of these ideas over a period of 2 to 3 years can result in a 40% reduction of non-value effort, scenario 1 vs. scenario 3. Almost more important you will have a complete set of x-rays and cat scans of your development process and economics. Your failure rate will materially decline. You will get a much better return on your software investment.

Longer term these measures (and others) can be leveraged with methods such as Lean and Six Sigma to initiate and monitor performance based improvements that will move you into the elite 15%.

You can do this! It's not rocket science and you don't need a million dollars to start!

[1]http://www.nytimes.com/2009/08/30/weekinreview/30pennebaker.html

[2]According to Webster's, "the agency, function, or office that acts as a substitute for another"

[3]See International Function Point User Group ("IFPUG") http://www.ifpug.org/publications/manual.htm - an ISO Standard

[4]Park, Robert E., et. al.. "Software Size Measurement: A Framework for Counting Source Statements". Technical Report CMU/SEI-92-TR-020. http://www.sei.cmu.edu/pub/documents/92.reports/pdf/tr20.92.pdf

[5] www.Hexawise.com

[6]http://www2.computer.org/portal/web/csdl/doi/10.1109/MC.2009.253

[7]A variety of definitions of "Cost of Quality" or "Cost of Poor Quality" are in use – some add "Prevention" as fourth category in addition those I use here. Some distinguish between internal failure and external failure costs. I believe this simplified approach is a good place to start, but do not rule out further refinements over time.

[8]This segment is based on an article I co-authored with Karl Williams. http://www.stsc.hill.af.mil/crosstalk/2007/02/0702gackwilliams.html

[9]Metrics and Models in Software Quality Engineering, 2nd Ed. p.258-259

[10]Shigeo Shingo, Study of "Toyoda" Production System for an Industrial Engineering Viewpoint, Productivity Press 1981

Glossary

Appraisal - Any activity whose principal purpose is to find defects. Includes a variety of testing and other pre-test methods such as formal inspections and static analysis.

ACE - Appraisal Containment Effectiveness - The percentage of defects present that are removed by a specific Appraisal type.

Benchmark - A point of reference such as averages, means, and distributions derived from industry studies of actual results.

Process Maturity - A rating, generally on a 1 to 5 scale, that characterizes the extent to which an organization uses defined and repeatable processes appropriate to the domain of activity. Established scales include those defined by Philip Crosby, by the Software Engineering Institute, and by ISO Standard 15504.

TCE – Total Containment Effectiveness - The percentage of software defects removed prior to release of software for customer use. (defects found pre-release) / (defects found pre-release + defects found post-release).

Defect - Any exception or deficiency in software sufficiently important to justify correction. Defects are often classified as "Major" (Severity 1 or 2) or "Minor" (Severity 3 or 4).

Defect Severity: 1 – Software does not run

2 – Major function disabled

3 – Minor function disabled

4 – Cosmetic error

Defect Potential - An estimate of the number of defects likely to have been "inserted" (present) at a given point in the development process.

Value-Added Effort - The percentage of total effort NOT devoted to Prevention, Appraisal, or Rework.

Rework - Any effort devoted to correction of defects both pre- and post-release.

Embedded Software - Software included within (as part of) another product not sold as software per se.

Package Software - General purpose software not developed solely for a specific customer.

TQM - Total Quality Management

Six Sigma - A process improvement methodology focused on reduction of defects and variance. Developed at Motorola during the 1980s.

Lean - A set of tools and concepts focused on reduction of waste and cycle time. Derived from the Toyota Production System.

Lean Six Sigma - In practice ideas from both have largely merged into a unified approach to process improvement, cycle time reduction, and elimination of waste.

SEI - The Software Engineering Institute. Established at Carnegie Mellon University. Initially funded by the US Dept. of Defense to focus on improvement performance of government software contractors. Authors of the Capability Maturity Model Integrated and several variants thereof.

CMMI® - Capability Maturity Model Integrated

Prevention - Any activity intended to reduce defect insertion and related rework. Typically includes training and process improvement initiatives.

Cost of Quality - A system of measurement that focuses on distinguishing non-value-added activities (primarily Appraisal and Rework) from value-added activities.

Agile Methods - A family of approaches to software development that attempt to embody Lean principles and practices.

Function Points - A software sizing method defined by the International Function Point User Group (IFPUG)

Critical Path Method - An "industrial strength" approach to project planning.

Earned Value - An "industrial strength" approach to project status reporting. Defined by an ANSI standard.

Bibliography

Barry Boehm, *Software Engineering Economics*, Prentice Hall (1981), ISBN 0-13-822122-7, (and Richard Turner) *Balancing Agility and Discipline: A Guide for the Perplexed*, Addison Wesley (2004) ISBN 0-321-18612-5

Capers Jones, *Software Engineering Best Practices: Lessons from Successful Projects in the Top Companies*, McGraw-Hill (2009), ISBN-13: 978-0071621618

Applied Software Measurement 3rd Ed., McGraw-Hill (2008) ISBN 978-0-07-150244-3

Estimating Software Costs 2nd Ed., McGraw-Hill (2007) ISBN-13: 978-0-07-148300-1

Assessment and Control of Software Risks Prentice Hall (1994) ISBN 0-13-741406-4

Frederick Brooks, *The Mythical Man-Month: Essays on Software Engineering 2nd Ed.*, Addison Wesley (1995) ISBN-13: 978-0201835953

Karl Wiegers, *Peer Reviews in Software*, Addison Wesley (2002) ISBN0-201-73485-0

Larry Putnam and Ware Myers, *Five Core Metrics*, Dorset House (2003), ISBN 0-932633-55-2

Peter Senge, *The Fifth Discipline: The Art and Practice of the Learning Organization,* Doubleday (1990) ISBN 0-385-26094-6

Robert Grady, *Successful Software Process Improvement,* Prentice Hall (1997) ISBN 0-13-626623-1

Practical Software Metrics for Project Management and Process Improvement, Prentice Hall (1992) ISBN 0-13-720384-5

Ron Radice, *High Quality Low Cost Software Inspections,* Paradoxicon (2002) ISBN 0-9645913-1-6

Stephen Kan, *Metrics and Models in Software Quality Engineering, 2nd Ed.,* Addison Wesley (2003) ISBN 0-201-72915-6

Tarek Abdel-Hamid and Stuart Madnick, *Software Project Dynamics* Prentice Hall (1991) ISBN 0-13-822040-9

Tom DeMarco, *Controlling Software Projects,* Yourdon Press (1982) ISBN 0-917072-32-4 (with Tim Lister) *Peopleware: Productive Projects and Teams,* Dorset House (1987) ISBN 0-932633-05-6

W. Edwards Deming, *Out of the Crisis,* MIT CAES (1982), ISBN 0-911379-01-0

Watts Humphrey, *Managing the Software Process,* Addison Wesley (1989) ISBN 0-201-18095-2

A Discipline for Software Engineering, Addison Wesley (1995) ISBN 0-201-54610-8

Winning with Software: An Executive Strategy, Addison Wesley (2002) ISBN 0-201-77639-1

IEEE Std 1028™-2008 IEEE, 3 Park Avenue, New York, NY 10016-5997, USA

Meet Gary Gack

Gary Gack is an MBA from the Wharton School, a Six Sigma Black Belt, and an ASQ-certified software quality engineer. He provides consulting, training and coaching related to business and software/IT process improvement, with emphasis on "best of breed" integration of proven best practices and models.

Software and IT projects, like Black Holes, consume vast amounts of time and money, yet often do not deliver what was promised, are frequently late and over budget, and are many are defect prone when deployed. Sometimes not even light comes out! Outright failures are quite common and can have serious consequences for careers and for the bottom line. Outsourcing has produced decidedly mixed results. Organizations continue to take a trial and error approach with little systemic improvement noted. Dramatic improvements are possible, but require a combination of sustained best practices - silver bullets simply don't exist, as evidenced by the absence of dead wolves!

Learn more about Gary at: www.process-fusion.net